Do *You* Have What It Takes to Run a Business?

Leonard J. Pellman

ISBN: 979-8-85-235151-7

LIONHEART
PUBLICATIONS

San Antonio, Texas

DEDICATION

To Nneka L. Cleaver, founder and CEO of Black Business San Antonio, who provided the inspiration and impetus for this book's creation and the business incubator in which its content was previewed, critiqued, applied, and refined prior to its publication.

CONTENTS

INTRODUCTION

I've been an entrepreneur—a "serial entrepreneur" in fact—for over 55 years now. And that's even if you don't count the time I spent mowing lawns, washing windows and cars, operating a lemonade stand, and selling candy bars door to door as a child. I bought my first business in 1967, when I was 15 years old, and I've owned and operated some sort of business (often as a side-business) ever since ... nineteen of them at last count.

A couple of those businesses have been spectacular successes, most have been moderately successful, and a couple have also been dismal failures. Each of them has been a learning opportunity.

In addition to that practical hands-on experience, I have an MBA and a PhD in Management, and I served as a professor and assistant dean of Business, Economics, and Leadership for twenty years at a major midwestern university.

What I've gleaned from those experiences is that America's business schools **don't** ... **won't** ... and **can't** teach you the most important aspects of entrepreneurship and running a business. The reason for this is simple: **the majority of teachers and textbook authors don't know how to run a business**, so they really can't teach anyone else how to run a business.

Most college professors and textbook authors have spent their adult lives merely reading and writing book reports about running a business. A few have personally interviewed a few business managers, primarily CEOs of multinational corporations who rarely perform the pick-and-shovel work of running a business. But it is extremely rare to find one who has actually operated a business for any significant length of time.

As a result, most business textbooks and college courses

are filled with high-minded theories and platitudes, but contain little practical insight into the daily grind of running a business. This book was written to fill that void.

The US Small Business Administration has for decades pointed out that more than ninety percent of all new businesses fail within their first three years of operation. Nevertheless, despite the SBA spending hundreds of millions of dollars per year on education, training, and support of small businesses, as well as issuing billions in small business loans, that statistic hasn't changed in over 40 years. Why? Because the bureaucrats at the SBA don't know how to run a business, either. They only know the rules imposed by the federal government on businesses and what they've read in textbooks. The SBA can tell you *what* a business must do to succeed, but not *how* to do it.

This book, and the self-assessment workbook I created to accompany it, explain what you need to know to run a successful business, the skills you must possess as the principal manager of a business, and the attitudes that highly successful entrepreneurs all possess. I call them "KSAs" as a shorthand for *knowledge*, *skills*, and *attitudes*.

The SBA and most textbooks claim that the reason most new businesses fail is that they are under-capitalized, meaning they didn't have sufficient funding to sustain their operations until they began turning a profit. On the surface that seems logical, since most businesses that close do so because they run out of money.

Well, that's what happens to most failed businesses, but it's not the **reason** they run of out money. In most cases, a business runs out of money because its owner(s) didn't have the **KSAs** to properly plan, organize, and manage it. If they had the KSAs to thoroughly research and plan the startup and growth of the business, they would have known how much working capital they would need to sustain it until it became profitable and would have ensured that sufficient capital was available.

It may sound as if I'm trying to talk you out of starting a business, but I'm actually trying to do just the opposite; I'm trying to prepare you to succeed at launching your business and spare you the grief of being just another tragic statistic among those 90% who opened their doors without the tools—the KSAs—to accomplish their dreams and vision.

I know from personal experience how painful it is to have your dreams and ambitions come crashing down around you. After you've put your heart and soul into creating and launching a business, it is devastating to watch your dreams, months or years of toil, and usually a huge amount of your money, and/or money you've borrowed from family and friends, all go up in smoke. So I'm going to spend the next 100+ pages doing my utmost to spare you that heartache.

The ideas I've presented in this book, don't come exclusively from an American cultural perspective, either. I've been blessed and privileged to live and work among people from many cultural backgrounds: European, Middle Eastern, African, Asian, Pacific Islander, and Hispanic. My business practices have long been a blend of the best lessons I could learn from each. And I'm still learning.

If you glanced at the table of contents, you already know that the book starts at ground zero with the most fundamental of all fundamentals:

- What is a **business**?

- What are the major **functions** of a business?

- What is an **entrepreneur**?

- What is **management**?

- What **KSAs** do you need to be an entrepreneur or manager?

I think it's important to build your understanding from the bedrock up, so you have a clear comprehension of *what* a business really is, *why* you're really doing it, and whether or not you already have the KSAs to succeed or if you need to develop some additional KSAs as part of the process of planning and starting your business.

For good reason, the first of the three maxims inscribed in marble at the Temple of Apollo at Delphi around 600 BC was *"Gnothi seauton"*—**Know Thyself**. If you know yourself well— candidly acknowledging your strengths and weaknesses, virtues and vices, abilities and limitations, knowledge and nescience, impartialities and prejudices—you have already formed the foundation for success in business.

1

WHAT IS A BUSINESS?

The dictionary says a business is (1) "an occupation, profession, or trade" or (2) "a person, partnership, or corporation engaged in profit-seeking enterprise." Both of those definitions are absolutely correct, but most people don't realise that **whatever activities you perform to sustain your life is a business**. Specifically, *your* business.

Read both definitions again. A business is not just a brick-and-mortar store or a legal entity. Flipping burgers at a fast food restaurant is "an occupation, profession, or trade." Begging for food on a street corner is "an occupation, profession, or trade." Buying and selling things at yard sales is "an occupation, profession, or trade." Owning and running a nail salon is "an occupation, profession, or trade." It doesn't matter whether we are working as an individual, a partnership, a corporation or LLC, whatever work we do is a form of business.

It's only a "job" or "labour" if we don't treat it like it's our business.

So, the first task of any and every entrepreneur is to treat the work they do as a business, rather than a job or merely labour. It must be your **occupation**, meaning the activity that occupies the majority of your time and attention. It must be your **profession** and therefore performed with virtuosity. And it must be a **trade**, meaning that you take an active role in seeking out and developing its markets, customers, resources, and business associates.

And that brings us to the next question: **What is the purpose of a business?**

Most business textbooks will give you the right answer: "**to maximise the value of the owner(s)' interests.**" The problem with that textbook definition is that most textbooks and professors do a terrible job of explaining the two vital most vital concepts expressed in that sentence: **value** and **owner(s)' interests**. As a result, even many people with business degrees, along with nearly everyone without a business degree, believe the purpose of a business is to make a profit or to maximise the business profits.

They couldn't be more wrong.

Although every business must make a profit—which means profit must be an essential component of every business plan, budget, and forecast—making, or even maximising that profit does not necessarily maximise the value of the owner(s)' interests. In fact, as we will see in Chapter 3, profit should actually be treated as an *expense*—an essential cost of doing business—rather than a goal of the business.

Value and profit are two different things, as I also explain in Chapter 3, so here I'll focus on the concept of owner(s)' interests.

Most business textbooks define owner(s)' interests as their share of the ownership in the business based upon its net worth or equity (its total assets minus its total liabilities). So, if I own 25% of a business with assets of $100,000 and liabilities of $60,000, its net worth or equity is $40,000 and *my* interest in the business is 25% of that or $10,000.

But that only describes the *financial* aspect of my interests in the business. Your full interests in a business can—and for most people should—be much broader than that.

For instance, a popular topic (and buzzword) these days is "generational wealth" or "legacy wealth" that can be passed on to your children, then to their children, and so forth. But passing on a business that your children are not willing or able to manage may not be the best way to create that generational wealth for your descendants. In that case, it may be more desirable for the business to provide another way for its accumulated wealth to flow to your descendants.

Or perhaps you started your own business so that you wouldn't be tethered to a 40-hour work week 50 weeks of the year on a job, but could have more freedom with your time, even if it requires sacrificing some of the profits to hire a manager to run the business whilst you enjoy that leisure time. Or you may have started the business in order to give you the opportunity to travel the world as a legitimate business expense. Don't discount the notion of personal satisfaction, either. One of your life goals may be to build the best mousetrap ever invented or provide the best service or personal care ever offered. Your business may very well be, at least in part, an outlet for your artistry and creativity. And you should consider using the business to build a retirement fund large enough to sustain a comfortable (or even lavish if you wish) lifestyle to at least age 90.

Those are just a few ways in which your interests in the business can be much more than just the equity it accumulates. To maximise **the value of your interests** in the business may involve striking the right balance **for you and your family** between its accumulated equity, your leisure time, flexible work hours, travel, generational wealth for your children, creative drive, community service and charitable work, retirement goals, and much more. Those interests must be viewed holistically, not just monetarily, and should encompass all the reasons you started the business; not just its monetary results.

Accordingly, before you pick a name for your business, before you sign a lease or hang the "Open" sign on the door, **you must decide what life goals and ambitions you want your business to achieve for you**. Although it will seem like it at times, your business is not your life. It is a method by which you accomplish and finance many of your life's goals and ambitions.

To better understand the relationship between you and your business, it may help to consider what it means to be an entrepreneur.

Entrepreneur is a word borrowed from the French language. It means "**one who undertakes**" [a task, mission, journey, etc.]. You probably didn't know that running a business would make you an **undertaker**, did you? In English an entrepreneur is usually understood to be "a person who organises and manages an enterprise." We'll examine the concept of an enterprise in more depth later, but for now think of it as any form of business or organisation (including charities, political groups, non-profits, social clubs, schools, sports leagues, etc.) that serves people or provides products.

Therefore, an entrepreneur is anyone who treats the work they do as an enterprise and applies sound economic and managerial principles to that work. An employee or labourer is someone who treats the work they do as a job, and relies upon their employer or boss to manage their work and the results it produces.

The purpose and function of an employee is to achieve the *employer's* dreams and ambitions. **The purpose of being an entrepreneur is to achieve *your own* dreams and ambitions.** Remember that, because it becomes important when your business begins hiring employees, agents, and/or contractors.

So, the first step in running your business is to view yourself as an entrepreneur and act accordingly.

To succeed in creating and running an enterprise, an entrepreneur needs several critical **KSAs** (Knowledge, Skills, and Attitudes). KSA is a term you should become familiar with, because it applies to every aspect of running a business.

What KSAs Do You Need?

Knowledge

- Thorough Industry Knowledge
- Fundamentals of Economics

- Basic Marketing Principles
- Solid Arithmetic (including some basic algebra) Ability
- Basic Probability and Statistics
- Fundamentals of Finance and Financial Management
- Fundamentals of Production & Operations Management (i.e., workflow)
- Fundamentals of Business Law (especially contract law and HR law)
- Basic Psychology (particularly the five fundamental human needs)

Skills

- Communication Skills (strong reading, writing, and persuasion skills)
- People Skills (active listening and dialogue, empathy, relational skills)
- Administrative Skills (organising, record-keeping, policy making)
- Accounting Skills (basic GAAP, tax reporting, cost accounting)
- Computer Skills (especially website and business software)
- Managerial Skills (planning, organising, and controlling activities)
- Creativity and Problem-Solving Skills (good analytical skills)
- Leadership Skills (especially servant-leadership)

Attitudes

- Positive Outlook
- Entrepreneurial Mindset
- Mission-driven
- Passion, Vision, and Commitment
- Uncompromising Devotion to Excellence
- Self-control and Personal Discipline—"The Grind"

- Personal Integrity, Trustworthiness, and Sincerity
- Benevolence, Justice, and Compassion
- Iron Will

That sounds like a lot, doesn't it? Well, **as an entrepreneur, the success of your enterprise depends almost entirely on you**. As the business owner and/or manager, *you* establish the benchmarks of professionalism that your employees will follow and your customers will experience. *Your* abilities and attitudes will define those of your business.

So, yes, you *do* need a lot of KSAs.

In the chapters that follow, each of these essential KSAs is explained in more detail, both to help you understand why each is needed to run a successful business and to help you determine the extent to which you presently possess or lack each one.

Most so-called "experts" will tell you that 90% of all new businesses fail because they are under-capitalised, meaning they didn't have enough money to sustain the business until it began turning a profit.

Those "experts" are wrong.

The real reason that 90% of new businesses fail is because their owners or managers **lacked the KSAs to realise that they were under-capitalised**. The lack of capital wasn't really the problem; the lack of the KSAs to know how much capital the business would need and to secure that capital before opening its doors was the problem.

I have personally witnessed this scores of times. The entrepreneur came up with an idea, possibly even a great idea, rented the least expensive building they could find, created a website and/or social media page for the business, printed some business cards and fliers, told everyone they knew they had started a business, and put a "Now Open" sign in the window. And they were shocked that customers weren't lined up around the block waiting to buy from them.

Everyone they knew told them it was a great idea and would sell like hotcakes. But, all too often not even their friends and family actually purchased their products and services. They go on paying rent, utilities, insurance, telecommunication charges, etc., only to watch their products gather dust until they run out of money. And they wonder what went wrong.

Tragically, most entrepreneurs devote less time and effort to planning their business startup than to planning a vacation. They open their doors without truly knowing their market, their operating costs, their competitors, or even their break-even point. The result is a financial and emotional disaster.

In order to better understand the KSAs that are necessary to successfully run a business, it may be helpful to review the basic functions every business must perform.

2

BASIC BUSINESS FUNCTIONS

There are five major functions that every business must perform:

- Marketing
- Finance
- Operations/Production
- Administration
- Accounting
- Management

MARKETING

Marketing entails every aspect of informing potential customers about your products and services and persuading them to buy from you. The textbook term for this is the "marketing mix," often called "**the Four Ps** of marketing."

Traditionally, the Four Ps were: Product, Price, Place, and Promotion, but I personally believe there are two more elements of the marketing mix that must be addressed by every business: People and Processes. I will explain my reasoning as I describe each of these factors.

Product is whatever you sell to your customers. It includes everything your customer receives as part of the transaction— the physical products, services, and packaging.

For a restaurant, the product is not only the food and

beverages that customers consume, but also the atmosphere and ambience of the premises, the services provided by the staff, the table settings (linens, dishes, flatware, etc.) the customers use, the to-go containers, gift wrapping ... basically everything the customer uses whilst dining or takes home with them.

In a nail salon, the product is also a combination of products (artificial nails, nail polish, skin care products, etc.) and services (application of the nails, trimming and shaping, hand massages, and so forth). If the salon offers complimentary items, like free coffee, tea, champagne, or valet parking, those are included in **product**.

For every business, **the real product is ultminately** *customer satisfaction*.

Price is what it costs the customer to purchase your product and/or service. It is not merely the amount listed on the menu or price tag, but also includes taxes and other costs (tips, parking, registration or licensing fees, postage or delivery) that customers incur to do business with you.

A factor many business people fail to consider when pricing their products and services is *convenience*. But customers do weigh the cost, in both time and expense, of traveling to and from your place of business. That's what keeps convenience stores in business. People will pay $2.99 for a bag of chips at a convenience store rather than drive 10 or 15 minutes out of their way and stand in a longer line at a grocery store to purchase the same bag of chips for $1.79.

Place is therefore a vital aspect of marketing, because it impacts elements of both price and product. Place is where your business transactions occur, whether it's at a brick-and-mortar store, a website, in the customer's home, or other location. Place is vital, because it affects the accessibility of your products to customers, the public image of your business, and the cost of doing business with you.

Promotion is everything you do to make customers aware of your business and persuade them to buy from you. It includes all forms of advertising, free samples or other give-aways, prizes and contests, publicity, personal appearances, trade show displays, sales presentations, building signage, discounts, coupons, and incentives, customer and investor communication, and tie-ins with other businesses or events.

People. Your people, especially their *attitudes*, are a vital element of the marketing mix. Unless your business is conducted entirely online, your people are both literally and figuratively the "face" of your business. So, their appearance and professionalism is a major part of the public image and marketing of your business. And your people aren't just the ones you hire directly, but any agents, contractors, or vendors who come in direct contact with your customers. If you use a call centre in India to provide customer service, then Rakesh or Bhakti in the call centre are *your* people as far as your customers are concerned, and you must manage how they interact with your customers and how they affect the image of your business. If UPS delivers your products, then the UPS driver is one of *your* people as far as customers are concerned.

Processes, as used here, refer to both the processes by which your products and services are provided to the customer (hand made versus machine made, for example) and any "back office" functions that customers come in contact with, such as billing and collections, complaint resolution, and quality control. A customer may be thrilled with the widget they buy from you, but if the invoice is inaccurate or the warranty is mishandled you may lose that customer forever. Conversely, a timely thank you card or call could save a customer you might otherwise lose.

Although people and processes could be considered aspects of product, and are treated as such in some textbooks, I believe they are important enough to receive separate and equal consideration and effort with product, price, place, and promotion.

Marketing is everything. And it's the only thing.

Read that again: Marketing is *everything* and it's the *only* thing. Everything your business does affects how customers perceive your business and must be treated as part of your marketing mix. As a business owner and manager, you are marketing your business from the moment you turn the key or log in to the moment you turn off the lights or log out.

Of course, none of these are independent of each other. All four or six Ps are connected and must enhance each other ... what textbooks call "integrated marketing." You don't sell Piaget watches out of the back of a 1985 Yugo unless you want your customers to think they're stolen. And you don't sell shabby knock-offs in a marble-floored store lit by crystal chandeliers and expect your customers to pay top dollar for them. Your product, price, place, promotion, people, and processes must all reinforce each other and present potential customers with a consistent and favourable image of your business and its products and services.

FINANCE

Every business needs money in order to function. Finance is the effort involved in securing funds for your business. It includes direct investment in the equity of the business, loans and grants from third parties, credit arrangements with suppliers, investments, and generation of adequate profits from operations.

Financing the business must be one of its highest priorities and a key element of the overall business plan and marketing plan. Yes, how the business acquires its working capital is part of marketing since it has a profound affect on the cost and quality of its facilities, products, and operations.

The form of business—sole proprietorship, partnership, corporation, etc.—can have a significant effect on the financing methods available to a business, so finance must be a key consideration when deciding the form in which to organise your business. Some of the common business structures in the United States include:

- Sole Proprietorship
- Partnership (general or limited)
- Corporation (including Subchapter S)
- Limited Liability Company (LLC)
- Limited Liability Partnership (LLP)
- Non-Profit Corporation

Each of these business structures has advantages and disadvantages to its owners in terms of taxation, owners' liability, regulation and reporting, record keeping, and financing, so choosing the right structure for your business is critical to its success. **It is a decision that should be made *only* after consultation with your legal, financial, and tax advisors.** The descriptions below are provided solely for informational purposes and are not intended as advice as to which is best for your particular business.

Sole Proprietorship. This is simply *you* operating as your business, either under your own name or by filing an assumed name (such as Len's Auto Care), also known as a "DBA" (doing business as) with the appropriate agency in your state or county of residence. A sole proprietorship is usually the simplest and least expensive form of business organisation to establish. Since there is only one owner, no formal documents are required to create a sole proprietorship other than a DBA if it uses a name other than yours, but it has several drawbacks. It offers no protection against liability, so if someone is injured whilst doing business with you, they can sue *you* personally for their damages. All the income from the business is reported and taxed to you personally, which can reduce your taxes if the business suffers a loss, but drastically increase your taxes if it is profitable.

A sole proprietorship raises money from contributions by its owner, loans, lines of credit, grants, or credit from suppliers. The credit of the business is based on the creditworthiness of its owner.

General Partnership. In most states a general partnership is treated the same as a sole proprietorship, except that it has more than one owner. In most states the partners are not required to create a written partnership agreement, but it is highly recommended to minimise the potential for disputes. It only needs to file a DBA for the assumed name it will use. However, it also has all the disadvantages of a sole proprietorship regarding taxation and personal liability of the owners. In order to document the division of the partnership's income (or loss) between owners, a partnership will have to file a Form 1065 Partnership Tax Return with the IRS and usually an equivalent form with the state. Each partner must be provided with a Form K-1 showing the allocation of profit or loss for inclusion in their individual federal and state tax returns.

A partnership raises money from contributions by its partners, loans, lines of credit, grants, or credit from suppliers. The credit of the business is based on the creditworthiness of its partners as a group.

Limited Partnership. Most states also permit a company to be formed as a limited partnership in which one or more of the partners is a general partner and others are treated as limited partners. As the name suggests, limited partners have limited liability and are basically investors only who receive a share of the profits of the partnership as prescribed in the partnership agreement and have little or no say in the management of the business. The general partners bear most of the liability, as well as the responsibility for managing the business, just as they would in a general partnership. Due to the need to protect the interests of the limited partners, a limited partnership usually involves a greater administrative and accounting burden on the general partners, as well as certain fiduciary responsibilities.

A limited partnership receives its initial funding from the investments made by its limited partners. The general partners rarely use their own money to finance the venture. It can also receive funding from loans, grants, lines of credit, or extension of credit from suppliers.

Corporation. A corporation is an entirely separate entity from its shareholders, as implied by the word "corporation" ("embodiment"). To create a corporation, its organisers must file Articles of Incorporation and By-Laws with the Secretary of State in the state in which they wish to domicile the business. Once organised, a corporation raises its initial capital by selling shares to the public. Those shareholders elect a Board of Directors to manage the business, and the Directors in turn elect officers (at minimum a president, secretary, and treasurer) to conduct the day-to-day management, subject to review by the Directors.

The administrative and accounting burden on a corporation is significantly greater than on sole proprietorships or partnerships in order to comply with the By-Laws and state and federal regulation of corporations.

In addition to the money raised by the sale of shares of stock, corporations can also take out loans and lines of credit, apply for grants, and be extended credit by suppliers. The credit of a corporation is based upon its creditworthiness as a distinct entity; not on the credit of its shareholders, although closely-held corporations with only a few shareholders must often provide lenders with personal guarantees from officers, directors, or major shareholders.

A corporation with fewer than 100 shareholders, all of whom are individuals, estates, or certain types of trusts, may elect to be treated as a "**Subchapter S**" corporation by the IRS. This can alleviate some of the regulatory burden, but it also imposes a number of restrictions on the organisation.

Limited Liability Company. A form of business created in the latter 20th century is the limited liability company (LLC). An LLC blends features of a corporation and a sole proprietorship or partnership. It is a separate entity for legal and tax purposes, and its owners enjoy limited liability, but its record keeping and reporting requirements are less onerous than for a corporation. It does require a formal certificate of formation, however. An LLC can elect to be treated as a Subchapter S corporation for federal tax purposes, so it affords its owners more flexibility than a corporation with most of the protections provided by incorporating.

Limited Liability Partnership. An LLP is a business structure available in most states that blends the features of a general partnership, limited partnership, and LLC. It is treated as a partnership for tax purposes, but like an LLC in most other ways. It requires a formal organising document to be filed with the Secretary of State, and all of its partners are treated as limited partners. It is most commonly used by professional offices like doctors, dentists, lawyers, engineers, and accountants.

Non-Profit Corporation. You don't have to lose money to be a non-profit (termed a not-for-profit in some states) corporation. In fact, non-profit organisations tend to be much more profitable than most for-profit businesses. The key difference is how they are taxed and how they must keep their accounting records. In addition, a non-profit must be established for one of the purposes your state permits. Usually those purposes are educational, recreational, social, or charitable. So if you a starting a business that provides education or training, recreational activities, social services, or support for a charitable cause, it may be advantageous to create it as a non-profit corporation.

However, there are also significant disadvantages to a non-profit. Any wealth the corporation accumulates must be donated to charity if the business closes, and there are strict accounting regulations that apply to non-profits, and the organisation cannot engage in profit-making activities that are not directly related to the non-profit activities stated in its charter.

Each type of business structure has advantages and disadvantages for the owners, so choosing the most beneficial structure for your business is one of the first, and most important, decisions you must make in starting or acquiring a business. It is highly recommended that the type of organisation for your business be decided in consultation with your legal, tax, and financial advisors.

Once your business has been formed you can begin seeking financing for it. If you organised as a corporation, you can sell shares of common stock to investors. If you formed a sole proprietorship, you will be the only direct investor. As a partnership or LLC other people can invest directly in the business, but you will be sharing ownership, decision-making, and any profits made with those additional investors. You can also finance your business, regardless of its legal structure, with loans, lines of credit, grants, or trade credit.

Before you begin raising capital, however, you will need to know how much capital you need to raise in order to launch and successfully operate your business. To calculate the funding needed for your business, you will need to know how to perform several basic financial calculations, including break-even analysis, internal rate of return, principal and interest computation, payback period, and more.

OPERATIONS/PRODUCTION

Operations, sometimes called production or production and operations, is a general term for the activities a business performs in providing its products and services. Typically, the operations function includes any and all manufacturing, shipping and receiving, inventory control, storage and warehousing, loss prevention, maintenance and repair, quality control, customer service, safety management, and operational security.

ADMINISTRATION

Administrative functions common to most businesses include policies and procedures, record keeping, claims and complaints, human resource documentation and reporting, legal issues, contract administration, regulatory compliance and reporting, information management, internal communications, and risk management.

ACCOUNTING

Accounting involves keeping the financial records of the organisation, taxation, budgeting, and financial controls. Every business needs an accounting system that provides its manager(s) with up-to-date, accurate, and useful information about its financial activities. The better the accounting system, the more likely the business will be to succeed.

MANAGEMENT & LEADERSHIP

Management, as the term is used here, refers to planning and forecasting, organising and coordinating workflow, problem solving, crisis and internal dispute resolution, control of business activities, research, development, and continual improvement of products and services. Leadership is the component of management that involves such interpersonal skills as influencing, persuading, and networking, as well as setting the overall attitude, ethics, values, and culture of the organisation.

CROSS-FUNCTIONAL DISCIPLINES

In addition to the functional activities of a business described above, a business manager needs to develop at least moderate proficiency in a number of cross-functional disciplines and skills, including:

Mathematics. Everybody hates maths! Even at the graduate level, on the first day of class fully two-thirds of my students in Statistics, Accounting, Economics, and Finance courses would ask, "There isn't going to be a lot of maths in this course, is there?" Strangely enough, "It's almost entirely maths" wasn't the answer they were hoping for.

Unfortunately, the bedrock of all business analysis and decision making is maths. Nearly every business decision involves some sort of arithmetic or mathematical calculation, so get used to the idea now. The better you are at maths the better you will do in business. At the very least you should be proficient in addition, subtraction, multiplication, division, with the ability to correctly apply the order of operations (aka PEMDAS) and solve basic binomial algebraic equations.

Economics. There is much more to economics than just the Law of Supply and Demand. The word "economics" comes from the Greek words "*oiko nomikos*," meaning to **manage one's livelihood**, so the discipline of economics provides tools and formulae for managing every aspect of life—business, family, leisure, … everything.

In the immortal words of Professor Pellman: "*Every* decision you make in life is an *economic* decision. So equip yourself to make the best decisions you can."

Statistical Analysis. A statement often misattributed to Mark Twain is, "There are three kinds of lies: lies, damned lies, and statistics." Although politicians routinely use statistics to deceive voters and criminals use statistics to deceive investors, when used properly statistics are a powerful tool for helping entrepreneurs manage their businesses.

Business Law. There are literally *millions* of laws currently in effect. In fact, there are so many laws now in effect that our government can't even count how many there are, much less know what they all say and how they apply. Yet, somehow **you must run your business in a way that complies fully with every single one of those laws!**

Yes, it's an impossible task, but you have to do it anyway. Fortunately, most of those millions of laws fall within a few overall principles, so if you know the fundamentals of contract law, tax law, HR law, and tort law you can avoid 99% of the major legal pitfalls.

Communication. All of marketing, and the most important aspects of all other business activities involve communication. It is therefore essential that business owners be effective communicators. The success of your business will be determined primarily by how effectively you can communicate your ideas verbally and in writing, and how well you can understand what others communicate to you.

Psychology. Every business exists in order to solve people's problems and meet their needs. You therefore need a basic understanding of psychology in order to be able to convince customers to buy your products and services, investors and lenders to provide the funds your business needs, and to persuade your employees, agents, or contractors to perform their work proficiently.

Every human being has these five fundamental needs:

- Security
- Significance
- Intimacy
- Innocence
- Hope

The success of your business is built upon how effectively you can meet one or more of those basic needs for your customers, employees, investors, lenders, and other constituents.

Security. We all need to feel physically, emotionally, and spiritually safe, stable, and reasonably secure. We need a sense that our well-being is not in immediate or significant jeopardy.

Physical security includes such things as food, clothing, shelter, job security, and safety from harm. Emotional security is a sense of contentment or happiness, freedom from anxiety and worry, and lack of drastic mood swings. Spiritual security is having a general sense that our life has meaning and purpose, and that life itself is precious.

Significance. Everyone has a powerful need to feel important and valuable in some way. We want our lives to matter, to make a difference, to be worthwhile. This is true of ourselves as entrepreneurs, of our customers, our suppliers and vendors, our investors, and our employees.

Intimacy. We are designed to be in relationships, so we have a strong need for some of those relationships to be completely open and honest. We need to know that someone truly cares about us and wants a personal relationship with us. We need a few relationships in which we can reveal our deepest thoughts, desires, and fears without worrying that we will be judged or outcast for them.

Innocence. We all long to feel blameless. Each of us has a need to believe that we are a good person, that our actions are ethical, moral, justified, and righteous.

Hope. Above all else, people need hope. Hope is the wellspring of life itself. We need a reason to believe that our problems, pains, and sorrows won't last forever, that every new day has the potential to be better in some way than the one before.

Of course, there's a lot more to psychology that just these five basic needs, but they are a solid starting point for developing a better understanding of your customers, employees, vendors, and even yourself. Everyone has these five fundamental needs, so if you can address them in a positive way when dealing with people it can help tremendously in avoiding and resolving conflicts. If people are unable to meet these needs in a beneficial way, they will meet them in a detrimental or harmful way instead.

As you define, design, and plan your business, it will be

helpful to keep these five human needs in mind and frequently ask yourself how doing business with you will meet one or more of these needs for your customers, employees, lenders, vendors, investors, and associates.

3

BUSINESS & ECONOMICS

As I stated earlier, **every decision you make in life is an** *economic* **decision**. Every single one. If you think there is any decision you make that is not economic in nature, then you don't yet understand economics well enough to be starting or running a business.

The concept of economics comes from the Greek words, *oiko nomikos*, which translates literally as "household management." But, prior to the 20th century a "household" was not merely a residence or a group of people all living under one roof. When the term *oiko nomikos* was coined by the ancient Greeks, **a household was an enterprise** that included all of one's possessions, relationships, and activities—the home, family, servants and employees, friends and advisers, investments, and income-producing activities.

In other words, **your "household" is everything that sustains your life** and livelihood. So, *oiko nomikos* (economics) is the process of managing your life. And the field, discipline, and practice of **Economics entails applying scientific methods to managing your life more effectively and successfully** (however you choose to define success).

The essence of economics, therefore, is determining what actions or decisions produce the greatest **value** (benefit) or **utility** (usefulness) to your household (your enterprise). Neither value nor utility is necessarily measured by money or money alone. Personal satisfaction, self-esteem, quality of relationships, self-expression, and anything else that is important to you is, and should be, included in determining the value or usefulness of your actions and decisions.

This is why many entrepreneurs are willing to work for less than the lawful minimum wage. They value their freedom, independence, or creativity more than they value the additional money they could make working for someone else. So every economic decision is highly personal and individual. There is no one right answer that applies to everyone.

You don't need to be an "expert" in economics in order to manage a business, but there are some basic economic principles that every entrepreneur should understand.

Supply and Demand. The most fundamental concept of economics is supply and demand. Supply (the amount of something that's available) and demand (how much of something that people want) are the forces that govern all economic activity. As a general rule, the more of something that's available relative to the demand for it, the lower its price (value) will be and the less of something there is relative to the demand for it, the higher its price will be.

Air provides an excellent illustration of supply and demand. Everyone needs air in order to live, so demand is extremely high. But on 90% or more of the planet's surface, air is readily available in large quantities with almost no effort to obtain, so in most places on earth we can all breathe for free.

However, at the peak of Mt. Everest the air is so thin that it doesn't provide enough oxygen to sustain life, so it must be compressed and packaged in metal tanks and breathed through a regulator and face mask that require effort and expense to make and fill. If you wish to climb Mt. Everest (and live to post the pix on social media), you must purchase or rent the air and the equipment to transport and breathe it. Although it's the same commodity, the location and conditions of its use alter its value to you.

The term economists use to describe conditions in which there is the demand for something is greater than the supply is **scarcity**. And scarcity usually increases the price or value of an item if there is demand for it. Certain little pieces of rock, like diamonds, rubies, gold, and platinum are more expensive than other rocks like quartz or granite or iron because they are scarce.

In 1905, at the age of 13, my grandfather went to work full time as a blacksmith's apprentice, learning how to shoe horses and repair buggies, carriages, and wagons. By the age of 16 he had his own blacksmith's shop and was earning a middle class income. But by 1917 he had closed his blacksmith's shop and was working as a barber, because the automobile had made blacksmiths all but obsolete. In 1905 a blacksmith's skills were scarce and still in high demand, so they could earn a good living, but ten years later the supply far exceeded demand and a blacksmith could barely get enough work to make ends meet.

This example illustrates not only how supply and demand affect the price or value of a product or service, but also to point out that the conditions affecting supply and demand are constantly changing. Products, services, and skills that are scarce or in high demand today may be plentiful or in low demand tomorrow.

Price Elasticity. The economic term for how strongly the market reacts to changes in price is "price elasticity." It is a vital concept for every business owner and manager to understand. If sales of a product or service drop significantly in response to a price increase or rise significantly in response to a price decrease, the demand for that product or service is highly **elastic**. If sales change little in response to price increases or decreases, demand is said to be **inelastic**.

Who Determines Price? If you answered "The business manager," you are wrong.

The concept of price elasticity answers this question for you, because it is actually **your customers** who ultimately determine the price of your products and services based on their individual *perception* of the value and utility to them of those products and services. I often use the example of my custom hand-crafted artisan toothpicks to illustrate this concept.

I make custom hand-crafted artisan toothpicks out of the

rarest exotic hardwood from Yabbadoo trees that I grow myself in the nutrient-rich soil on the eastern slope of an extinct volcano on a private island off the western coast of Sumatra, which is the only place in the universe where Yabbadoo trees can grow. The island alone cost me $100 million. Each tree takes 40 years to grow under the careful cultivation of a team of 27 of the world's most foremost horticulturists who are paid an annual salary of $120,000 each. Out of each mature tree I harvest, I use only the perfect wood from its exact centre for my toothpicks, and a typical tree yields only enough of that wood for four or five toothpicks. It costs thousands of dollars to fly to Indonesia and take a chartered boat to my private island to harvest a tree, and six weeks of my labour, ten to twelve hours a day to whittle each toothpick to perfection by hand. I spent 44 years as an unpaid apprentice to the world's greatest toothpick whittler to learn and perfect my craft, and no one in the world possesses similar carving skills to mine. When I'm done, my total cost is $482,763.51 per toothpick just for the raw materials and transportation, but I'm willing to charge only a pittance for my unparalleled skills and labour, so I've priced each toothpick at only $500,000. When you factor in what my labour, training, creativity, and artistry are truly worth, I'm barely breaking even at that price!

So, how many of my artisan toothpicks will you buy today? None?! What if I offer a 5% discount on a dozen and a 10% discount on a box of 100. *Now* how many do you want? Still none??? Don't you realise how rare both the materials and my artistry are? Surely, you must agree that my toothpicks are worth at least twice what I'm charging. Probably more like five times that amount. So, why aren't you lining up to buy them?

Simple. They're not even worth a penny to you, because all you want is something to pick a little bit of gristle out from between your teeth. 99.9% of the people in the world don't care how much my toothpicks cost to make, how rare and expensive Yabbadoo wood is, or how much of my life I've devoted to become the greatest toothpick carver in history. They don't think any toothpick, no matter how rare or perfectly carved, is even worth a dime, much less half a million dollars. Sure, a couple billionaires and maybe a toothpick museum will pay handsomely just to possess a one-of-a-kind work of art, but no one else will. Not if they're sane.

That's because **value and utility are personal perceptions;** not absolutes. **How much a customer will pay for a product or service has almost nothing to do with the cost or skill involved in producing it** and everything to do with what the buyer thinks it's worth to him or her. Basing your prices on your costs and what you believe your skill, talents, and creativity are worth is a surefire formula for business failure.

The price of your products or services must be based upon what the customers who have access to them are willing and able to pay. And that means you have to understand your market.

What is profit? Another term that even many economists don't fully understand is "profit."

Most people think that profit is income minus costs. It's what you have left after you've deducted all your costs from the sales you've made. That's how the dictionary and even some textbooks define it: "the pecuniary (monetary) gain remaining to a seller of products or services after deducting all of their costs."

Well, yes and no. It's not technically incorrect, but it's the wrong way to think about profit. GAAP (Generally Accepted Accounting Practices) provide a hint about the right way to think of profit. Under GAAP, revenues (income) are treated as credits in a company's books and expenses are treated as debits. Profits, which GAAP calls "net income," are also debits.

In other words, net income (financial profit) is treated as an expense, and that's exactly how entrepreneurs should think of profits. **Profits are the most important expense a business incurs** and should be central to your business plan and budget, because profits are all that sustains a business and allow it to grow.

Unfortunately, instead of making net income the first and foremost expense of their businesses, many entrepreneurs treat their profits more as an afterthought, hoping there's some profit left over after they've paid all their other bills. They would never treat their rent, mortgage, utilities, or employee wages this way, because they know they'll be evicted, have their power shut off, or lose their employees if they do. So they make sure they generate enough revenue to provide for those expenses in full to keep their doors open. And they should be doing the same with net income—their profits.

How much profit does a business need? The answer to that depends upon the nature of the business, its mission, vision, plans, and goals, and the purpose for which its owner(s) created it. A business that requires continual high investment in equipment and facilities or is seeking rapid growth needs higher profits than a business with lower investment needs or intends to grow slowly and steadily, for example. That's why a clear, detailed, and realistic marketing plan or business plan (see Chapter 4) is necessary from the outset.

What is money? When most people hear the word "economics" they think of money. Hopefully you now realise that money is not all there is to economics, but it is a vital component of economics and a concept every entrepreneur must understand.

Money is a "medium of exchange," a tool that facilitates trade between people and organisations. If we didn't use money, then people would have to directly exchange the things they make or the services they provide for the goods and services other people provide. For example, if I grow apples and you make chairs, I would have to trade some of my apples for one of your chairs. We might agree that one of your chairs is worth 50 of my apples, but what if you can't eat all 50 apples before 30 of them spoil? Then you would have to quickly trade those 30 extra apples for something else you need, like some tools. That complicates the exchange and alters the value to you of my 50 apples.

Money solves that problem.

If I pay you $50 for one of your chairs instead trading you 50 apples for it, you can go buy 10 fresh apples, some tools, and a new shirt—things that are of greater value to you than an overabundance of apples.

The convenience of money in facilitating trade between people and organisations can actually increase the desirability of many transactions and thus increase the value (and profits) of the goods being exchanged.

Money isn't the goal; **it's a tool** to help achieve your goals. It has no real value of its own. It's merely a symbol of the value available for your use and a convenient way to store that value. **It's what you acquire with money that has actual value to you.** You can't survive by eating money. You can't drive a pile of money to the store. Money won't keep you warm or keep the rain off you. Staring at a stack of money isn't very entertaining. But money can buy you food, a car, clothing, a house, heat and air conditioning, concert tickets, or a home entertainment system.

What is wealth? The word originated as a term for "wellness" just as "health" originated from "healed." Originally, health and wealth were two sides of the same coin, so to speak, one side meaning to be well and the other being healed after having been unwell. Over the centuries the two words diverged in meaning somewhat, so that "wealth" now implies being rich and "health" being physically or medically sound.

The science of economics has taken that meaning one step further and defined "wealth" as **the total of a person's or organisation's property and possessions plus the net present value (NPV) of their future earnings**. That's a perfectly sound way to calculate your wealth, but not a particularly good way to conceptualise it, since wealth isn't merely the sum of one's possessions.

An entrepreneur should think of wealth as **economic wellness** in much the same way we think of health as being physical wellness. Just as a person can be physically strong and active, but still have life-threatening chronic diseases like hypertension, diabetes, COPD, or even cancer and be far from healthy, businesses can have robust sales, plenty of assets, and still not be truly wealthy. So **entrepreneurs should make it a major goal to sustain and increase the wellness of their businesses** to avoid having to later heal from having been chronically unwell. A key component of economic wellness is earning profits that are adequate to achieve the objectives and sustain the growth of the organisation.

How is wealth acquired? Another huge misconception about wealth is that if one person or organisation accumulates enormous wealth it deprives another person or organisation of that wealth. In a free society (what most would call a "capitalist" society), wealth is neither found nor distributed; **it is created**. It is created by human ingenuity and effort. Today's mega-rich entrepreneurs, like Bill Gates, Elon Musk, or Mark Zuckerberg, didn't gain their billions by robbing nations of their natural resources, fleecing unsuspecting people, or exploiting their workers. They earned their wealth by creating and selling products and services that enriched their customers, their employees, and society.

A chunk of iron ore buried deep in the ground isn't wealth. It's doing nothing beneficial for anyone in its natural state. In order to be useful, it must be dug out of the ground and smelted to become a useful iron ingot. That alone involves considerable effort and expense, but it's just the beginning, because there's little use that can be made of a raw iron ingot, so it still has little value in that form.

You've probably seen the popular meme stating that an iron ingot sells for only about $5.00, but if you make it into horseshoes it will sell for $12.00. If it's fashioned into needles it's price increases to $3,500. And as watch springs it will sell for $300,000. Thus, its value is not in the material itself, but in the value of the objects that can be made from it or the uses to which it can be put by human ingenuity and effort. The more useful, desirable, and scarce the end product is, the higher its price will be.

The same is true of salaries and wages. The more valuable and desirable the work performed is, the higher the wage or salary is for doing it. Someone who flips $2.00 hamburgers will be paid a fraction of what someone who can make a million dollars a day in the stock market will be paid. It's not the effort required or the difficulty of the work that establishes its value, nor is it the amount of education or training required to perform the work. It's what the end consumer is willing to pay for the merchandise or service the work produces and the scarcity of those with the KSAs to do that work that ultimately determines an employee's wages.

The miracle of economics. That's what I call it. In every voluntary transaction, both parties—the buyer and seller—make a profit. Read that again. Drill it into your mind. In a voluntary transaction, meaning neither the buyer nor seller is being coerced into it, **both make a profit**. That's the miracle of a free market.

If I make a hamburger that costs me $4.00 to make and you buy it for $5.00, not only do I make a profit of $1.00 on the sale, but you also make a profit of some amount on the purchase. You don't "lose" $5.00; you gain a hamburger that's worth more to you than $5.00. If you weren't convinced the hamburger was worth more than the $5.00 you paid for it, you were insane to buy it. So, assuming you're sane, you bought it because you profited by the purchase. Perhaps not a monetary profit, but you gained something—speed, convenience, personal satisfaction, etc.—that was more valuable to you than the $5.00 you spent.

Not only did you profit personally by buying that hamburger from me, but the people I employed to cook and serve that burger also profited from your purchase, as did the vendors who supplied the bun, condiments, meat, grill, cooking utensils, and the building my burger joint leases. So the profits are spread throughout our society, as well.

That miracle—the profit that each participant earns—is what makes possible the vast array of products and services available today. Think what it would take for you to make a hamburger all by yourself. You would need at least one cow for the meat, plus enough land for that cow to graze and the grass or feed for it to eat. You'd need to grow wheat for the bun, lettuce, tomato, onion, and cucumber, and a mustard plant, all of which take months of tending to grow. You would need a tree for firewood and clay to build an oven. It would take months of preparation to obtain all the ingredients, then hours of work to make the dough, bake the bun, butcher the cow, grind the meat to make a patty, make the condiments, cook the meat, and assemble the finished hamburger. And if you wanted salt and pepper on it, you'd need a salt mine and a pepper tree.

To make one hamburger completely from scratch could easily cost you a million dollars.

Or you can go down the street to my hamburger stand and buy one for half an hour's wages. The amount of cooperation and social benefit that economic profits create is almost unimaginable. It often crosses borders and even oceans to make affordable products and services possible. And, as an entrepreneur you are an integral part of that miracle!

Yes, **every entrepreneur is a miracle worker**.

When you sell a product or service in a voluntary transaction, the profit you make is a reflection of the benefit that product or service provides to your customer, and an objective indication of the amount of good you have done for society. How do I know this? Because your customers willingly paid you for those products and services, which means they are convinced your products and services are worth that much to them. If they didn't think your merchandise was worth the price, they wouldn't have paid that much. It's that simple.

The bottom line is that **as a business owner or manager you will be making economic decisions every day**. The only question is whether or not you have the proficiency in economics to make good decisions or bad ones.

Now that you have an overview of the functions of business, the role of an entrepreneur, and the basic economic principles that will determine the success or failure of your business, it's time to get down to the nitty-gritty of starting and running an enterprise.

And the best place to start is with a plan.

4

BUSINESS PLANNING

Plan Ahead. Plan your work, then work your plan. Prior planning prevents poor performance. If you fail to plan, you plan to fail.

We've heard the cliches about planning all our lives and we all know the importance of planning. Nevertheless, most entrepreneurs spend more time and effort planning their family vacation than they spend planning their business endeavors.

It takes a lot more than a great idea to launch a successful business. The old adage, "Build a better mousetrap and the world will beat a path to your door" is an outright lie. It has never happened and it never will happen. Build a better mousetrap and no one will know or care that you've done it, unless you show or tell them you've done it and convince them that it really is better than other mousetraps.

To reach those potential customers you need to know who they are, where they are and where they prefer to shop, why the mousetraps they're using now are unsatisfactory, what features they most need in a mousetrap, when they plan to replace them, how you can get their attention. After you've discovered all that, you need to create or purchase the products you intend to sell them, a location in which to store and display those products, a marketing campaign to convince them to buy from you, financing to keep the doors open until your business turns a profit, and a system to keep track of everything you're doing.

And for all that you need a plan.

Some call it a business plan; others call it a marketing plan. Since (as you now know) everything a business does is marketing, the two are synonymous. I prefer to call it a **comprehensive business plan** as a reminder that a good plan addresses every facet of your business. At a minimum, a comprehensive business plan should include the following:

1. **Business Name**. A memorable name that reflects your business concept.

2. **Brand and Image**. Branding is more than just the business name and logo. It's how people, including customers, employees, suppliers, and non-customers perceive your business.

3. **Business Concept**. A description of the general idea for your business in a couple sentences or a paragraph.

4. **Mission & Vision Statement**. What are you trying to accomplish with this business?

5. **Market Research.** A thorough analysis of the market for your products and services.

   a. **Market Size** (total dollar or unit sales of similar products and services)

   b. **Target Market Share** (the proportion of the market you expect to attract)

   c. **Market demographics** (age, income, spending, preferences, etc.)

   d. **Market trends** (growing, shrinking, stable, ...)

   e. **Market Economics** (supply and demand curves, price elasticity, competitors and substitutes, etc.)

6. **Competitive Analysis.** A thorough analysis of the competitors and substitutes in your market.

   a. Number, size, market share, and longevity of competitors and substitutes

   b. Competitors' market strategy, marketing mix, pricing structure, promotions

   c. Market leaders and competitors' growth trends

7. **Marketing Goals.** The revenue, profit, unit sales, and market share you plan to achieve by specific target dates (1st 90 days, break-even point, 1st year, 3 years, 5 years, etc.), and why those goals are attainable.

8. **Marketing Strategy.** A detailed description of how you will achieve your marketing goals.

   a. **Marketing Mix** (the 6 P's mentioned above)

   b. **Marketing Budget** (how much it will cost to execute your strategy, and over what time frame those costs will be incurred)

9. **Financing Plan.** How you will raise the capital needed for your business.

   a. **Sources of Funds** (personal investment, loans, venture capital, grants, etc.)

   b. **Repayment Plan** (for any and all loans and credit)

   c. **Operating Budget & Forecasts**

   d. **Capital Structure** (equity versus debt)

10. **Operations Plan.** How you will operate the business.

    a. **Staffing Plan** (employees, independent contractors, etc.)

    b. **Training Goals and Methods**

    c. **Policies, Procedures and Processes**

    d. **Business Licensing and Regulatory Compliance**

    e. **Communication Methods & Systems**

    f. **Quality Control & Improvement**

    g. **Facilities & Equipment**

    h. **Maintenance & Repair**

9. **Administrative Plan.** How you will perform all the necessary administrative functions.

    a. **Record Keeping & Reporting** (sales records, inventory records, HR records, safety records, legal records, meeting minutes, policies and procedures, regulatory compliance records and reporting, etc.)

    b. **Accounting & Taxes** (books of account, tax returns and returns, credit reports, budgeting, financial controls, etc.)

10. **SWOT Analysis**

    a. **Strengths** (advantages your business has over most of your competitors)

    b. **Weaknesses** (disadvantages your business has compared to most of your competitors)

    c. **Opportunities** (ways your business can exploit or benefit from market conditions that your competitors cannot)

    d. **Threats** (ways market conditions could harm your business that won't affect your competitors as badly)

Perhaps the most difficult aspect of developing a business plan is understanding and quantifying the market for your products and services.

When I first started in business, market research involved traveling to libraries, chambers of commerce, and government offices to wade through volumes of magazines, microfilmed records, and books to gather the information needed. It took weeks, often months, to obtain market data. And by the time it was published in print, much of that data was obsolete and no longer accurate. Now, anyone with Internet access can peruse mountains of data in a matter of minutes.

With that in mind, here are some questions you should ask and answer in order to gather the basic market data needed for a business plan:

1. **What is your type of business?** Be as specific as you can. Don't say "restaurant," if you're going to open a taco shop, soul food restaurant, Chinese restaurant, steak house, vegan, seafood restaurant, home style family restaurant, pizza delivery service, dessert shop, snack bar, cafeteria, all-you-can-eat, fast food franchise, etc. Is it upscale, self-service, drive-through, kid-friendly, specialty, or appealing to a particular demographic (teens, seniors, car enthusiasts, or certain ethnic groups)?

2. **What products and/or services do you (plan to) sell?** For a restaurant, will it be a limited menu (say, tacos only, steaks only, shish kebabs, etc.) or a full-range menu. Will it have a special service or feature, like cooking at the customers' tables teppanyaki style or cooked over flowing lava?

3. **Who are your primary customers?** Will it appeal to everyone, or will it cater to one or more specific groups (ethnicity, income, profession, hobbies or interests, tourists, etc.)?

4. **What is the geographic area of your market?** Even if your business is entirely online, there still may be practical

limitations on its geographic reach. Can you actually deliver your products or services to Antarctica, Inner Mongolia, or Bulawayo timely and affordably? Will people really drive 30 or 60 minutes to shop in your store? Probably not for take-out food if they want it to still be hot when they eat it. So, make sure the geographic scope you envision for your business is feasible.

5. **What is the population of your market demographic?** This refers to the population within the geographic area of your actual market; not the entire population of your city, county, or state. There may be 100,000 Scandinavian-American women in your city, but if only 10,000 of them live within a 30-minute drive of your traditional Viking design nail salon, then that is the population of your market demographic.

6. **What is their average income?** You don't want to wait until you've invested $100,000 in a building lease, tenant improvements, equipment, insurance and utilities deposits, business cards and a website to look at the Census data and find out that Scandinavian-Americans are generally in the lowest 20% income group and only 2,500 of them in your market area can afford custom Viking-themed nail designs.

7. **How much do they spend annually on your type business?** Many trade associations, industry groups, and affinity groups keep statistics on annual average spending for various types of consumer goods. You may have to join one or more of these groups to get access to the information, but if the membership isn't too expensive it may be well worth it to find out that Scandinavian-American women only spend an average of $97 per year getting their nails done.

8. **How many direct competitors are in your market?** Direct competitors are businesses that sell products similar to yours. Of course, your Viking nail designs are absolutely unique and the best in the world, but every shop in your market area that sells any form of nail care is your direct competitor.

9. **What is your actual or expected share of your market?** You should estimate your probable market share as both a percentage of the total market and a monthly or annual dollar

amount. An important concept in determining market share is **Price's Law**, which has verified that 50% of every market is captured by the square root of the number of competitors serving that market. If you have 25 competitors, five of them capture 50% of the market; the other 20 do about 2.5% each. It is thus reasonable to assume that your market share your first year as the 26th competitor will be no more than the 2.5% currently captured by those in the bottom 50%.

10. **What is your expected annual business revenue?** This estimate should be based on your answers to questions 5 through 8 above. In my example, that would be 2.5% of the $97 per year spent by the 2,500 Scandinavian-American in your market area who can afford custom nail designs, or $6,062.50 per year.

11. **Is the annual business revenue sufficient to sustain your business?** In my example above, it obviously isn't. But it's much better to discover that before you invest $100,000 in the nail salon. And it doesn't necessarily mean the end of your Viking nail salon dream. Instead, it may just mean that you must alter your business concept and model to make it feasible.

If you don't know the answers to the questions above, then before you do anything else, find out those answers. Those are the most fundamental things you need to know about the business you are considering. Don't be embarrassed if you don't know the answers yet. Most people don't when they first think about starting or buying a business. But, one reason many of those 90% fail is that they didn't find out before they opened their doors.

If your answer to Question #11 is "no," you have some more thinking and planning to do before you file your DBA or LLC, much less hang your "Now Open" sign. You either have to change your business model, or change your business goals to align with the realities of the market for your products and services.

Your comprehensive business plan does not have to be highly detailed or complex, especially for a new business. It must simply address every facet of your business in enough detail and specifics to serve as a road map to its success.

Some areas of uncertainty can and should be built into your plan. For example, if you are planning to open a new smoothie shop, but you're not sure what flavours will be popular with your clientele, you might plan to offer a standard menu limited to the five most popular flavours nationwide plus a locally themed "Flavour of the Day" at a discount to test their popularity and add any flavour that sells more than a given amount to your regular menu.

A good business plan is flexible, like a travel plan. If a road is closed or a flight is canceled, you don't turn around and go home. You find an alternate route or a different airline. Running a business is like being a special forces operator: **you must improvise, adapt, and overcome** in order to accomplish your mission, because no endeavor goes entirely according to plan.

A study done by the US Chamber of Commerce showed that **companies that have a well thought out business plan succeed five times more often than businesses that have no plan**. But that same study showed that **businesses that altered their plans to reflect new information and lessons learned succeeded five times more often than businesses that stuck to their original plans**.

Up to this point, you know what a business is and you understand your role as an entrepreneur. You've determined the type of business you're going to run, you've created a structure (sole proprietorship, partnership, LLC, or corporation) for your business, you've done your preliminary market research and prepared your business plan ... There's just one more thing you need to do before you start implementing that plan.

You need to determine if you have the KSAs you will need to start and operate that business successfully, or if there are some vital KSAs you need to acquire or improve before you hang your "Now Open" sign.

It makes no sense to have a plan to acquire all the tools and equipment your business will need without an equally well-conceived plan to acquire all the tools and equipment (KSAs) you will need to run that business.

5

ESSENTIAL KSAs

Back in Chapter 1 I listed what I consider the most essential KSAs an entrepreneur needs in order to be successful. In Chapters 2 and 3 I reviewed the major functions involved in running a business and the disciplines entrepreneurs need in order to manage those functions. In Chapter 4 I presented the outline for a basic comprehensive business plan.

Hopefully, now that you have reached Chapter 5 you fully appreciate the need entrepreneurs have for a solid set of KSAs in order to competently manage an enterprise. So, in this chapter I will review those essential KSAs and describe them in greater detail.

As a reminder, those essential KSAs include:

Knowledge

- Thorough Industry Knowledge
- Fundamentals of Economics
- Basic Marketing Principles
- Solid Arithmetic (including some basic algebra) Ability
- Basic Probability and Statistics
- Fundamentals of Finance and Financial Management
- Fundamentals of Production & Operations Management (i.e., workflow)
- Fundamentals of Business Law (especially contract

law and HR law)
- Basic Psychology (particularly the five fundamental human needs)

Skills

- Communication Skills (strong reading, writing, and persuasion skills)
- People Skills (active listening and dialogue, empathy, relational skills)
- Administrative Skills (organising, record-keeping, policy making)
- Accounting Skills (basic GAAP, tax reporting, cost accounting)
- Computer Skills (especially website and business software)
- Managerial Skills (planning, organising, and controlling activities)
- Creativity and Problem-Solving Skills (good analytical skills)
- Leadership Skills (especially servant-leadership)

Attitudes

- Positive Outlook
- Entrepreneurial Mindset
- Mission-driven
- Passion, Vision, and Commitment
- Uncompromising Devotion to Excellence
- Self-control and Personal Discipline—"The Grind"
- Personal Integrity, Trustworthiness, and Sincerity
- Benevolence, Justice, and Compassion
- Iron Will

The first time you read that list it probably sounded like a lot of KSAs—perhaps too many. But now, hopefully you see the necessary for most or all of them. And, bearing in mind that, as an entrepreneur, the success of your enterprise depends almost entirely on you, let's review each of them briefly.

Knowledge

Industry Knowledge. You will need to understand the industry in which your business is engaged. To succeed in any business, your products and services must solve problems or fulfill needs in ways that are your competitors don't, so you must know your industry and the strengths and weaknesses (remember SWOT?) of your competitors and potential substitutes thoroughly. You need to the best sources of the equipment, supplies, and services required to operate your business. And you especially need to understand your market and the buying behaviour of your potential customers—how they select who they do business with, what problems they are trying to solve or needs they are trying to meet, where they look for information, how much they are willing to spend to meet their needs, and how strongly they react to changes in price and quality of similar products.

Economics. You don't need to have all the formulae for economic calculations memorised, but you certainly need to understand most of the fundamental economic concepts, like supply and demand, price elasticity, scarcity, marginal revenue, marginal cost, substitutes, and utility in order to make sound business decisions.

Marketing. Knowing that marketing is everything and the only thing a business does, you obviously need to understand and practice the fundamental concepts of marketing, such as the marketing mix (the "Six Ps"), integrated marketing, market research, and the psychology of marketing.

Arithmetic. Since almost everything about business operations is counted and calculated using numbers, you need a solid grasp of arithmetic fundamentals—including order of operations (PEMDAS)—at the very least. It will help immensely if you can also solve simple (binomial) algebraic equations (i.e., $3x - 2y = 19$). And that's just so you can make change, calculate sales tax, compute the monthly payment on a loan or line of credit, balance your business checkbook, and fill out your quarterly and annual tax returns. The better you are at maths, the more adept you will be at analysing and managing your business.

Probability and Statistics. There are a myriad of extremely useful analytical tools based on probability and statistics that can help you make more precise, accurate, and beneficial business decision if you have an underlying knowledge of the underlying principles of probability and statistics. There is also plenty of software available these days to perform the actual calculations for you, but they are only useful if you understand the principles on which they're based, so you can plug the right data into the formulae.

Finance. Before you decide how much to invest in your business, whether to bring in outside investors, venture capitalists, lines of credit or business loans, you need to be able to calculate how each of those will affect the profitability of your enterprise, and how much each will cost. Again, you don't need to have all the formulae memorised, because they're easy to find on the Internet, but you do need to understand the concepts underlying such calculations as principal and interest, amortisation and depreciation, rates of return, and more.

Is it better to buy a delivery truck, lease it, or just rent one when you need it? There are ways to calculate and compare the costs of each choice if you understand the underlying financial principles.

Production & Operations. POM (production and operations management) provides numerous ways to calculate production costs, worker productivity, production capacity (i.e., the staff, facilities, inventory, etc. needed to serve a given number of customers per hour or day), ideal inventory levels and re-order times, supply chain efficiency, and much, much more. And, as with most maths-based decisions, there are apps and software for performing these calculations, provided you understand their underlying concepts and uses.

Business Law. As soon as your business starts making a decent profit, every politician, bureaucrat, and other criminally-minded person will be trying to take as much of that profit away from you as they can. You therefore need to understand the fundamentals of business law—particularly business regulations and licensing, intellectual property (copyright and trademark) law, employment law, tax law, contract law, landlord/tenant law, torts (damages and injuries), usury, and bailments. With that understanding you can protect yourself and your business from the worst and most likely legal and regulatory threats using contracts, insurance, and other hedges against those pitfalls. Most importantly, a basic understanding of business law will help you realise when you need the assistance of an attorney to avoid a legal pitfall.

Psychology. People are weird. Much of their behaviour is irrational and often unpredictable. That's because most of our behaviour is emotionally driven; not logically driven. So every entrepreneur needs to understand as much as possible about human behaviour. The Five Fundamental Needs (security, significance, intimacy, innocence, and hope) are an excellent starting point, but the more you can learn about psychology the better you will be able to understand and relate to your customers and the better you will be able to inspire and motivate you employees, contractors, and vendors.

Skills

Communication. Communication is the backbone of business. Practically everything you do in business depends upon your ability to communicate effectively with your customers, employees, vendors, business associates, and the many bureaucrats whose actions all have a profound impact on your success.

Relational Skills. Relational skills are part psychology and part communication, but they include some specific abilities that may demand special focus to develop. One of these is active listening, listening for the purpose of understanding; not just listening to reply or defend your own ideas. Another is empathy, which is a form of intimacy in which you try to sense what someone is feeling in addition to understanding what they are saying. But the most important relationship skill is **respect** —treating others the way you want to be treated.

Administration. Essential administrative skills are planning and organising, keeping accurate, timely, and readily accessible records, and maintaining effective standards, procedures, and practices.

Accounting. Although accounting is a form of record-keeping, it warrants separate mention because it involves meeting specific government requirements and regulations, such as GAAP (generally accepted accounting principles), tax computation and reporting, and providing financial information to lenders, credit bureaus, and other third parties in addition to internal uses. Those internal uses, like profit and loss statements, cost analysis, and sources and uses of funds statements are absolutely vital to the success of any enterprise.

Computer Skills. Practically everything involves some type of computer these days, so entrepreneurs need to be able to use computers to perform transactions, access information, research on the Internet, communicate by text, email, VOIP, and social media sites. It is also helpful to have some familiarity with website construction and maintenance. There is also a plethora of business software available to help manage your business, if you possess the skills to use it.

Management. One of the most important managerial skills is delegation. Running a business entails more work than a single human being can possibly accomplish, so entrepreneurs must develop the ability to delegate work and ensure that it is accomplished. Establishing organisational culture, values, mission, and vision are also vital managerial functions requiring considerable thought and skill.

Creativity & Problem-Solving. I mention creativity and problem solving separately from other managerial skills, because they are part skill and part aptitude or talent. Both can be learned and practiced to a great extent, but both also involve a degree of innate ability or inclination. Some people are just more creative than others. They routinely think "outside the box" without trying. An entrepreneur must develop his or her creativity and problem-solving ability to the greatest extent possible.

Leadership. Like creativity and problem-solving, leadership is inherent to managerial functions, but it is a distinct skill, in addition to being a set of character traits (personal integrity, charisma, honesty, and trustworthiness in particular). Based upon my decades of observation of both effective and ineffective leaders, I'm convinced that servant-leadership is the best mode for entrepreneurs.

Attitudes

Positivity. First and foremost, you must maintain a positive outlook. You must see the potential good in every situation— even in failures, problems, and set-backs. If you make a huge blunder, you must not dwell on the harm it did or the difficulty in correcting it, but on how much better you and your business will be from the lessons learned and the improvements made to correct the mistake. Always focus on the glimmer of light; not the surrounding darkness, no matter how bleak things may appear. A positive outlook frees your mind to focus on solutions instead of dwelling on problems.

Entrepreneurial Mindset. Just being an entrepreneur doesn't automatically instill an entrepreneurial mindset in you. Being an entrepreneur isn't merely a job, nor even a career or profession; it is a calling. In fact, it is one of the highest callings to which a person can aspire. **Running a business is the most beneficial public service there is**.

Read that again, and meditate on it until you recognise its truth: running a business is the most beneficial public service there is. **Businesses create 100% of the world's prosperity and security**. Governments only rule and restrict people. Charities just distribute the things that businesses create. It is businesses —90% of them run by entrepreneurs like you—that produce all the goods and services that sustain, protect, and enhance human life.

Never forget that governments cannot create a better world; they can only rule, restrict, or destroy what citizens and businesses create. Likewise, charities can only give away what businesses create and donate to them. Only businesses and entrepreneurs can create a better world, so **as an entrepreneur, you must embrace that noble calling** and set your mind to achieving all that you and your business can do for the benefit of humankind.

Mission-Driven. Because entrepreneurship is a calling, you must be powerfully driven to achieve the mission and purpose of your business. Your customers, employees, suppliers, and the communities in which you operate are all depending upon you for the products and services they need to enjoy prosperous and fulfilling lives.

Passion, Vision, & Commitment. In order to fulfill your role as an entrepreneur and accomplish the mission and purpose for which you formed your business and are devoting the majority of your time, effort, and ingenuity, you must be passionate about it, have a clear vision of its impact in your community, and an unwavering commitment to its success.

Devotion to Excellence. No business is trivial. If you provide a product or service that people are willing to pay for, then you are fulfilling a need or solving a problem that is important. You are making people's lives better, so mediocrity is not acceptable. You must be steadfastly devoted to excellence, to making your products and services the best they can possibly be for the prices you charge.

Self-Control & Discipline. Self-control and discipline are like the two sides of a single coin. Self-control is stopping yourself from doing things you shouldn't do, and discipline is making sure you do all the things you should do. Running a business will produce endless frustrations and temptations. Self-control is essential to prevent you from succumbing to them. Running a business also entails numerous mundane tasks that must be performed every single day, so discipline is required to stay on task. Of the two, discipline is far more difficult to sustain.

Integrity, Trustworthiness & Sincerity. Sure, we have all encountered crooked and untrustworthy business people. And many of them do seem to succeed, sometimes immensely, by cheating and deceiving people. But eventually people do recognise the corruption in those businesses and they ultimately those their customers or are litigated or prosecuted out of business. The best way to ensure the success of your business and the loyalty of your employees, contractors, and suppliers is to operate your business with integrity, honesty, and trustworthiness. Similarly, people will eventually recognise any hypocrisy in your speech or behaviour, so you must be sincere in all your interactions with people.

Benevolence, Justice & Compassion. Generosity can be extremely dangerous to your business, as well as to the people to whom you are overly generous. That's why a combination of benevolence, justice, and compassion are vital to an entrepreneur. In business, as in all other aspects of life, "tough love" is what benefits people the most.

Often, simply giving people what they want or need is the worst thing you can do for them. As the old saying goes, "Give a man a fish and you feed him for a day; teach a man to fish and you feed him for a lifetime." In many cases, the best thing you can do for someone is to let them suffer the consequences of their poor decisions and attitudes.

Similarly, compassion is not the same as sympathy or empathy. Genuine compassion demands action; not merely emotion. And it requires those actions that are most beneficial as a whole—meaning beneficial not only to the recipient, but to society and everyone who is affected by that action.

For that reason, the samurai were trained not to think of right and wrong solely in terms of legal versus illegal, or a set of absolute standards, but to consider what is beneficial versus harmful in a broad context when determining the appropriate action to take. If my action primarily benefits only me or a person I wish to help, but it harms the interests of, or is unjust to, others members of the community or society at large, then it is not truly beneficial and it shouldn't be done.

Iron Will & Confidence. Entrepreneurship is not for the timid. In requires iron willpower and confidence to get up every business day and begin the "grind" once again. Day after day, week after week, month after month, and year after year.

For an entrepreneur, each day brings a new set of problems, difficulties, obstacles, set-backs, and frustrations. But facing and overcoming all those challenges can bring deep satisfaction, fulfillment, and even a sense of triumph at achieving what most people are too fearful, timid, or undisciplined to even attempt.

Each day that your business remains open should increase the confidence you have in yourself, your KSAs, and your business concept and its mission, vision, and values.

My long-time friend and former pastor, Dr. John C. Maxwell, is famous for saying, "**Your attitude determines your altitude**." My 55+ years of business experience echoes that fact. Everything rises and falls with our attitudes, so if we want our businesses to succeed we must maintain positive and inspiring attitudes that keep our customers coming back and our employees showing up for work every day. We can't afford to let up or let down for a second.

Not in front of our customers, employees, vendors, lenders, or the public, anyway.

But we do need frequent relief from the tremendous stresses of running a business. For that reason, every entrepreneur needs family and friends with whom they can unload their pent up frustrations, fears, and disappointments. No textbook will tell you that, but it's another crucial aspect of running a successful business.

Celebrate publicly. Let your customers, employees, suppliers, and associates celebrate your successes with you and give them all the credit they are due for helping you achieve those successes.

But keep your despair, anger, frustration, and disappointment private and share it only with those in your inner circle who will not judge or resent you for venting to them. Those rare people are priceless, and whether they know it or not, you must consider them part of your team and include developing them as part of your business plan.

6

ASSESSING YOUR KNOWLEDGE

Now that we have reviewed the essential KSAs needed to manage a business, it's time to assess the extent to which you already possess those KSAs, so that you can develop a plan to improve the areas in which you're deficient.

The purpose of this assessment is to determine the extent of your knowledge in the areas that are essential to running a successful business, so it's vital that you be honest with yourself in evaluating the extent to which you currently possess each type of knowledge.

I recommend getting a copy of the *Do You Have What It Takes to Run a Business Self-Assessment Workbook* that was created as a companion to this book. It will guide you step-by-step through the self-assessment process. If you choose not to obtain the workbook, I suggest making your notes on a separate sheet of paper.

Score yourself in each of the managerial KSAs in the tables below, then transfer those scores to the summary page at the end of this chapter using the following scoring system:

0 = **None** (you have little or no knowledge of this subject)
1 = **Meager** (not enough knowledge for any practical use)
2 = **Limited** (knowledge only of basic concepts)
3 = **Sufficient** (enough knowledge for everyday use)
4 = **Proficient** (enough knowledge to excel in its use)
5 = **Expert** (you could teach a college course in this subject)

Circle the number in the "Score" column that corresponds to the description in each table that best describes your current level of knowledge in each of the nine categories listed below.

Industry Knowledge

DESCRIPTION OF KNOWLEDGE & EXPERIENCE	SCORE
No prior knowledge or experience in the industry	0
Have worked in the industry, but not as a manager or owner	1
Up to 2 years experience as a manager or owner in the industry	2
2 to 5 years experience as a business manager or owner in the industry	3
6 to 10 years experience as a business manager or owner in the industry	4
More than 10 years experience as a business manager or owner in the industry	5

Your Score: _____

Having extensive knowledge of your industry is crucial to developing a useful business plan, conducting and evaluating market research, and managing the operation of your business. The higher your score in industry knowledge, the more likely you are to succeed.

Economic Knowledge

DESCRIPTION OF KNOWLEDGE & EXPERIENCE	SCORE
Little or no knowledge of economics	0

Understand the concept of supply and demand, but not how to calculate or estimate them	1
Understand major principles of micro-economics, but weak at calculations	2
Can calculate supply, demand, price elasticity, marginal cost, marginal revenue	3
Have a degree in economics or equivalent knowledge	4
Can teach economics at the college level	5

Your Score: _____

You will make economic decisions every day of your life, so the extent of your economic knowledge is a key factor in your success. However, for practical business purposes **a score of 3 or 4 is all that is necessary**.

Marketing Knowledge

DESCRIPTION OF KNOWLEDGE & EXPERIENCE	SCORE
Little or no prior knowledge or experience in marketing	0
1 or 2 years experience in sales, advertising, product design, or other aspect of marketing.	1
Understand the Marketing Mix ("4 P's") with more than 2 years experience in multiple facets of marketing	2
3 to 5 years experience as a marketing manager	3
5+ years experience as a marketing manager or degree in marketing	4

Can teach marketing at the college level	5

Your Score: _____

Even though marketing is everything and the only thing a business does, **a score of 3 or 4 is sufficient** for any entrepreneur. A score of 5 makes you better suited to teach marketing or work in marketing for a multinational corporation.

Arithmetic Knowledge

DESCRIPTION OF KNOWLEDGE & EXPERIENCE	SCORE
Struggle with addition, subtraction, multiplication, or division	0
No difficulty with addition, subtraction, multiplication, division, fractions, or percentages	1
No difficulty with addition, subtraction, multiplication, division, fractions, percentages, exponents, or PEDMAS ("order of operation")	2
Proficient at addition, subtraction, multiplication, division, fractions, percentages, exponents, or PEDMAS ("order of operation") square roots, exponents, absolute value, and basic linear equations ($2x - 15 = 5$)	3
Proficient in most algebraic calculations (linear, binomial, and polynomial equations), factorials, and linear programming	4
Proficient at algebra, plus some differential and integral calculus	5

Your Score: _____

I cannot overstate the importance of arithmetic competency

for an entrepreneur. A business owner or manager crunches numbers every day. For practical purposes, however, **a score of 3 or 4 is sufficient** for any small business manager.

Probability & Statistical Knowledge

DESCRIPTION OF KNOWLEDGE & EXPERIENCE	SCORE
Little or no knowledge of probability and statistics	0
Can calculate basic probabilities (rolling a six, drawing an ace, etc.)	1
Can calculate simple probabilities and conditional probabilities plus mean, median, and mode	2
Can calculate mean, median, mode, variance, standard deviation, skewness, curtosis, and correlation coefficient	3
Can perform linear regression, multiple regression, Chi-square, t-test, p-value, etc.	4
Can teach probability and statistics at the college level	5

Your Score: _____

We are inundated daily with probability and statistical information and claims. "Four out of five dentists recommend ...." "82% of Americans support ..." We use probability and statistics constantly, often without conscious thought, usually by just making a seat-of-the-pants guesses when we estimate things like the percentage of our customers who will purchase a given product or select one size or colour over another. The broader and deeper our knowledge of probability and statistics, the more accurately we can make those sorts of estimates. For practical purposes, **most entrepreneurs should score a 3 or 4 in their statistical knowledge**, but a score of 2 is adequate for many.

Financial Knowledge

DESCRIPTION OF KNOWLEDGE & EXPERIENCE	SCORE
Little or no knowledge of financial management	0
Understands balance sheet and income statement, liquidity, and a few basic financial ratios (debt-to-equity, profitability)	1
Can calculate a few basic liquidity, turnover, profitability, solvency, and efficiency ratios	2
Can calculate most ratios plus discounted cash flows, NPV, loan amortization, and compound interest	3
Can use Monte Carlo simulation, CAPM, IRR, WACC, Beta value, and similar tools	4
Can teach managerial finance at the college level	5

Your Score: _____

Nearly every business activity is measured and evaluated in financial terms, so the stronger your understanding of financial management concepts and tools, the more likely you are to succeed. Of almost equal importance to the success of your business is the ability to present potential investors, lenders, and grant providers with meaningful and accurate financial information in order to acquire the financing it needs.

To manage your business effectively, as well as to present its financial information persuasively to potential sources of financing, **a minimum score of 3** is desirable. And, even though you may not use more technical and advanced financial management tools like simulations, a score of 4 may provide a significant advantage in obtaining funds for your business.

POM Knowledge

DESCRIPTION OF KNOWLEDGE & EXPERIENCE	SCORE
Little or no knowledge of production and operations management	0
Understand facilities & capacity planning, inventory control systems, scale and scope	1
Understand the product-process matrix, life cycle planning, supply chain management	2
Can perform trend analysis, BPE and BPR, QC, PERT, MRP, queuing analysis, decision trees	3
Can perform linear programming, regression analysis, replacement analysis	4
Can teach production and operations management at the college level	5

Your Score: _____

This is one of my pet peeves about business education in America today. Because excessive regulation has forced most manufacturing overseas, most colleges and universities have removed production and operations management (POM) from their curricula, despite the fact that every business still has some form of production and operations. Since POM is literally *how to run a business*, I simply don't understand how a college can claim to award business degrees yet not teach POM. A knowledge of POM provides you with a tremendous tactical and operational advantage over all your competitors. **You can get by with a score of 2 or more**, but a score of 3 or 4 is preferable.

Business Law Knowledge

DESCRIPTION OF KNOWLEDGE & EXPERIENCE	SCORE

Little or no knowledge of business law	0
Understand basic concepts of contract law, employment law, and business regulation	1
Understand major principles of torts, civil law, criminal law, and administrative law	2
Understand agency, bailments, warranties, creditors' rights, implied contracts and breach	3
Competent at writing contracts, protecting real and intellectual property, tax law	4
Can teach business law at the college level	5

Your Score: _____

There are millions and millions of local, state, federal, and international laws currently in effect. So many, in fact, that the government can't even count them, much less keep track of them. Hundreds, perhaps thousands of those laws are conflicting, so that to comply with one you must violate another. Nevertheless, your business must fully comply with each and every one of them, and some of those laws are enforced by agencies you've never heard of until they knock on your door and fine or prosecute you for violating one of them. Not even a lawyer knows all the laws applicable to your business, but **you should at least score a 2 or 3 just to avoid major legal problems**. If you can't afford an attorney, you should probably score a 4.

Behavioural Science Knowledge

DESCRIPTION OF KNOWLEDGE & EXPERIENCE	SCORE
Little or no knowledge of psychology and sociology	0

Vague understanding of human perception, emotions, motivation, and social conditioning	1
Some knowledge of personality types (Meyers-Briggs, etc.), influence, and conformity	2
Understanding of bias, stereotypes, prejudice, false attribution, cognitive dissonance, OCD	3
Understanding of stress, phobias, depression, neuro-transmitters, somatic system	4
Able to teach behavioural science at the college level	5

Your Score: _____

Nearly every aspect of business involves human behaviour, whether it's dealing with customers and suppliers or supervising employees and contractors. To run a successful business requires a score of at least 2, preferably 3, and ideally 4.

Knowledge Self-Assessment Summary

Now that you have completed the knowledge self-assessment, **transfer your score in each category of knowledge into the Knowledge Summary Table** on the next page, or the similar table in your Self-Assessment Workbook, or a separate sheet of paper formatted like the table.

Whatever you do, **don't be discouraged** if your scores are not as high as you would like them to be. The reason you're taking this self-assessment is to ensure that you realise what knowledge you currently lack—knowledge you may need to obtain from consultants, professionals, or colleagues to avoid making major blunders whilst you are studying to improve those areas in which your knowledge is weak.

It's not that you shouldn't start or manage a business if you lack some critical knowledge; only that you should find sources for whatever knowledge you may not currently possess.

A description and outline of a KSA self-improvement plan is provided in Chapter 9.

Knowledge Summary Table

DESCRIPTION OF KNOWLEDGE AREA	YOUR SCORE	MIN. SCORE	IDEAL SCORE
Industry Knowledge		3	5
Economic Knowledge		3.5	4
Marketing Knowledge		3.5	4
Arithmetic Knowledge		3	4
Probability & Statistics Knowledge		2.5	4
Financial Knowledge		3	4
Production & Operations Knowledge		2	4
Business Law Knowledge		2.5	4
Behavioural Science Knowledge		2	4
KNOWLEDGE TOTALS:		25	37
**AVERAGE SCORES:		2.78	4.1

** For your average (mean) score divide your knowledge total by 9

If your average knowledge score is 2.5 or higher, you probably already possess enough business knowledge to start running a business, but you should develop an improvement plan to bring your overage average up to at least 3.0. If your score is 3.0 or higher, you definitely have enough knowledge to start and run a business, but you will probably benefit by raising your score to 3.5 or above.

Knowledge is a stage in a continuum, so it is typically developed by building upon the previous stages of the process. The four stages are:

Data. The raw facts.

Information. Data that have been analysed and conclusions drawn from it.

Knowledge. Information that has been compared to and combined with personal experiences to reach a deeper and more complete understanding.

Wisdom. Knowledge that has been tempered by compassion and moral principles to produce decisions and actions that benefit the broadest possible spectrum of society.

Now that you have an overview of your current business knowledge, you can evaluate the extent to which you have the business **skills** to apply that knowledge effectively.

7

ASSESSING YOUR SKILLS

In addition to having sufficient knowledge in essential business subjects, an entrepreneur also needs a vital set of business skills. In a nutshell, knowledge is knowing what to do and skill is actually being able to do it. It's the difference between knowing the recipe for a souffle and being able to make a souffle that doesn't collapse whilst it's cooking, has an appealing texture and appearance, and tastes great.

Knowledge can be acquired by reading, listening, and watching. Skills are learned by **doing**.

Score yourself in each of the managerial skills in the tables below and transfer your scores to the summary page at the end of this chapter in the same way you scored yourself in the knowledge factors in the previous chapter using the scoring system below:

0 = **None** (you have little or no skill of this kind)
1 = **Meager** (not enough skill for practical use)
2 = **Limited** (enough skill for basic business uses)
3 = **Sufficient** (enough skill for everyday business use)
4 = **Proficient** (enough skill to excel in business)
5 = **Expert** (enough skill to train specialists in this function)

Circle the number in the "Score" column that corresponds to the description in each table that best describes your current level of skill in each of the ten categories that follow below in this chapter.

If in doubt, err on the side of caution and select the lower of the categories that most closely describe you.

Verbal Communication

DESCRIPTION OF BUSINESS SKILL	SCORE
Limited vocabulary, timid about face to face sales or public speaking; dislike meeting new people	0
Average vocabulary, somewhat outgoing, but hesitant to speak to strangers or in public	1
Willing to meet new people and speak publicly, but not confident or eager to do so	2
Eager and confident meeting new people, solid vocabulary, at ease speaking publicly	3
Extensive vocabulary, eloquent and compelling speaker, highly persuasive and engaging, confident being interviewed	4
Experienced public speaker, large event host, or broadcast personality	5

Your Score: _____

You are the face and voice of your enterprise, so you must be able to comport yourself confidently with customers, employees, vendors and suppliers, investors and lenders, and the public at large. You should also seize every opportunity to be interviewed for radio, television, podcasts, and print publications. You don't have to sound like a college professor, news anchor, or Shakespearean actor, but you must be able to speak clearly, precisely, and persuasively in every setting in which you find yourself. **A score of 2 is probably sufficient** to start out, but **a score of 3 or 4 makes you fully equipped for business communication.**

The danger of a score of 5 is that speech that is too sophisticated can sound arrogant to some people. A haughty tone might work in an art gallery or literary society, but no in most businesses.

Written Communication

DESCRIPTION OF BUSINESS SKILL	SCORE
Little or no persuasive writing ability or experience	0
Limited writing skills, difficulty with spelling, grammar, syntax, and/or punctuation	1
Can compose letters, emails, or short essays with few errors	2
Experienced at composing business letters, marketing materials, and web content	3
Experienced writing technical specifications, complex instructions, lengthy essays, and/or detailed analytical reports	4
Published author of books, magazine articles, peer-reviewed papers, academic theses, or dissertations.	5

Your Score: _____

Much of your business communication is in written form, so you must have at least a good grasp of grammar, syntax, spelling, and punctuation in order to write clear, concise, and persuasive business letters, reports, emails, and advertising materials. You don't need to be a professional writer, but you do need to write well enough to be understood and to persuade your readers that you are a competent business manager. As with verbal communication, **a score of 2 is sufficient for the early stages of a business**, but **a score of 3 or 4 will provide you with significantly greater ability to convince investors, lenders, and vendors of your business acumen.**

People Skills

DESCRIPTION OF BUSINESS SKILL	SCORE
Indifferent to others' feelings, critical, gossiping, impatient or easily annoyed by others	0
Usually a sympathetic listener, supportive, helpful, but sometimes temperamental and argumentative	1
Active listener, compassionate, nurturing, patient, and understanding	2
Good negotiator and peace-maker, empathetic, collaborative, calm under pressure, and trustworthy	3
Good motivator, networker, persuasive, well-liked, respected, team-builder, and calm in a crisis or disaster	4
Creative problem-solver, crisis manager, charismatic, inspirational leader of large groups	5

Your Score: _____

Every business must relate to people. Customers, investors, suppliers are all human, so the better your relational skills, the greater the chances of your success. **A score of 2 is adequate for most daily interactions** with people, but for handling complaints, compliance audits or investigations, and conflicts with customers or vendors, **a score of 3 or 4 will better serve you**.

Administrative Skills

DESCRIPTION OF BUSINESS SKILL	SCORE
Few or no administrative skills	0

Not well organised, work not well planned, little or ineffective time management, seat-of-the-pants	1
Somewhat organised, but often distracted, uses to-do list but seldom completes it	2
Work well organised, prioritised, tightly scheduled, and usually completes tasks on schedule	3
Highly organised, does extensive research, meticulous record-keeping, plans months ahead	4
All work prioritised and structured, never misses an appointment, call, or deadline	5

Your Score: _____

Your ability to organise, schedule, and prioritise you own work, as well as the work of employees, contractors, and vendors is crucial to your success. There are only 24 hours in a day, 7 days in a week, and 52 weeks in a year. You should be sleeping at least 8 hours per day, destressing for a couple hours a day, and devoting a few more hours a day to your family and friendships. So, if you maintain a healthy work-life balance, you won't have enough time each work day to accomplish everything on your daily to-do list.

Therefore, administrative skills are crucial for every entrepreneur in more to ensure that you accomplish everything that is vital to the success of your business and only postpone or omit those actions and decisions that are of least importance and urgency. For that reason, **a score of at least 3 is recommended.**

Accounting Skills

DESCRIPTION OF BUSINESS SKILL	SCORE
Few or no accounting skills	0

Uses a simple cash-basis bookkeeping system containing minimal detail	1
Double-entry bookkeeping, following GAAP, but with only a balance sheet and P&L statement, basic sales and income tax returns	2
Detailed GAAP bookkeeping with cost of goods sold, cash flow analysis, depreciation and amortisation, ratio analysis, and complex tax analysis	3
Sophisticated accounting system with cost and profit controls, highly detailed reporting and analysis of operations	4
Capable of teaching accounting at the college level	5

Your Score: _____

If your business is generating fewer than 10 transactions per day, you may be able to manage it by simply monitoring your bank account and jotting down income and expenses in a notebook. But if your business begins to thrive, you must have some basic skills in accounting, so **a minimum score of 2 is an absolute necessity** for success, and **a score of 3 or 4 should be your goal** by the time your business has one or more employees or contractors.

Computer Skills

DESCRIPTION OF BUSINESS SKILL	SCORE
Few or no computer skills	0
Use computers for email, web surfing, and social media	1
Use computers for email, web, social media, blogging, word processing, and spreadsheets	2

Proficient in Word, Excel, PowerPoint (or equivalents), social media, blogging, and can create a basic static website	3
Competent with most business software, website coding, graphic design, video editing	4
Competent with a wide range of computer software, including coding and networks	5

Your Score: _____

When I bought my first business, only massive government agencies, universities, and major corporations could afford computers. My first computer cost $67,000 in 1976. It had a whopping 16 KB of RAM and two, yes *two*, 1.2 MB disk drives —less computing power than one of today's pocket calculators! But, I was still able to use that computer to out-compete all but my largest business rivals.

Today, computers are so commonplace that practically everyone and every business uses them. For $500 or less, anyone can buy a computer or cellphone with more than 1,000 times the computing power of my first computer. Even so, computers can still provide businesses with significant competitive advantage, if you know how to use them most effectively, and every facet of your business can benefit from the use of inexpensive software and apps and to not use a computer in your business is practically a guarantee of failure.

Thus, **a score of 2 in computer skills is an absolute minimum**, and **a score of 3 or 4 is far preferable**.

Managerial Skills

DESCRIPTION OF BUSINESS SKILL	SCORE
Few or no managerial skills, makes seat-of-the-pants decisions	0

Does some research before making decisions, but mostly guesswork and intuition, has supervised 2 or 3 people	1
Makes written research-based goals, plans, and decisions; verifies results personally, has managed teams of 5 to 10	2
Uses managerial tools like MBO, PERT, Six Sigma, decision trees, detailed research, reporting, and analysis, has successfully managed teams of 10 to 20 people	3
Has successfully managed teams of 20+ to accomplish complex and sometimes challenging goals	4
Has successfully managed teams of 100+ to consistently accomplish complex and challenging L/T goals	5

Your Score: _____

Management is the skill necessary to accomplish things. In entails planning, coordinating the efforts of everyone involved in achieving the objective to maximise their effectiveness and efficiency, monitoring progress and making necessary adjustments, solving the problems that arise, and ensuring that the outcome produces the desired results.

No business can succeed without competent management, so **a score no lower than 2 in management skills is necessary**, and the greater your managerial skills, the more likely the success of your business. It is impossible to be too skilled in management.

Creativity

DESCRIPTION OF BUSINESS SKILL	SCORE

Little or no creativity or imagination	0
Sometimes has new ideas or ways of doing things better	1
Always seeking and often finding new or better ways of doing things, highly imaginative	2
Frequently develops new or better ideas that prove to be practical and effective	3
Often develops trend-setting or breakaway ideas that are adopted by others or recognised as significant	4
Widely recognised as a creative genius	5

Your Score: _____

Creative thinking is the skill that allows you to offer goods and services that your competitors don't. It helps you see the opportunities that others miss. Of course, there is much creativity that can readily be hired from experts, particularly in advertising, store design and decoration, promotional ideas, website design, and even product development. But many entrepreneurs lack the funds to hire creative talent and must rely upon their own, at least in the early—and most crucial—stages of developing their businesses.

Also, a degree of creativity is needed to understand the creative ideas those experts provide and evaluate their viability for your business. Not every creative idea will appeal to those in the market for your specific products and services.

So you must have a few fresh and appealing ideas of your own, meaning **a score of at least 2**, and in order to continue improving your business and offering new products and services to your customers, **you should develop a score of 3 or higher**.

Critical Thinking & Problem-Solving

DESCRIPTION OF BUSINESS SKILL	SCORE
Few or no problem-solving or critical thinking skills, gullible and easily fooled	0
Takes most things at face value; occasionally verifies facts and information	1
Seldom accepts opinions without personally fact-checking and verifying information	2
Uses structured, objective research, analytics, and logic to verify almost all information	3
Uses scientific analytical methods to solve problems and make decisions	4
Could excel as a research scientist	5

Your Score: _____

Yes, critical thinking and problem-solving are both managerial skills, but they are so important to business success that I believe they merit special emphasis in your skills development.

Critical thinking is the ability to rationally, objectively, and dispassionately analysis things. In particularly, it is the ability to identify bias, subjectivity, and inaccuracies in the information you acquire in preparation for decision-making. Similarly, problem-solving involves identifying the actual root causes, of problems; not just the symptoms.

An effective entrepreneur needs a score of at least 2 on the above scale, and much preferably a 3 or 4.

Leadership Skills

DESCRIPTION OF BUSINESS SKILL	SCORE
Few or no leadership skills, rarely takes charge or is given leadership roles	0
Leads from authority or positional power, assertive or demanding, but not persuasive	1
People occasionally follow your advice or example, put you in charge, or ask your opinion	2
People frequently follow your advice or example, put you in charge, or ask your opinion	3
You are an effective, trusted, and recognised servant-leader	4
Highly admired leader with a following in the hundreds or thousands	5

Your Score: _____

Leadership is also a managerial skill. Not every leader must be able to manage people and activities, but every manager needs some effective leadership qualities.

Leadership is far more than merely acquiring cheerleaders who agree with what you say and will celebrate your successes. It is the ability to influence, motivate, inspire, and persuade people to take action—hopefully action that improves people's lives, benefits the community and society, and facilitates the operation of your business.

A score of 2 in leadership is sufficient for most simple interactions with customers and suppliers, but in order to manage employees and convince investors or lenders to finance your business, **a score of 3 or higher is essential.**

Skills Self-Assessment Summary

Now that you have completed the skills self-assessment, **transfer your score in each category of to the Skills Summary Table** on the next page, or the similar table in your Self-Assessment Workbook, or a separate sheet of paper formatted like the table.

As with your baseline knowledge, don't be discouraged from starting or managing your business if you lack some vital managerial skills. Just be sure your business plan provides for acquiring the additional skills you may not currently possess, and include ways you will develop those skills in your KSA self-improvement plan in Chapter 9.

Skills Summary Table

DESCRIPTION OF KNOWLEDGE AREA	YOUR SCORE	MIN. SCORE	IDEAL SCORE
Verbal Communication		2	4+
Written Communication		2	3+
People Skills		2	4+
Administrative Skills		3	4+
Accounting Skills		2	3.5
Computer Skills		2	3.5
Managerial Skills		2	3+
Creativity		2	3.5
Critical Thinking & Problem-Solving		2	3.5
Leadership Skills		3	4+

	SKILLS TOTALS:		20	36+
	**AVERAGE SCORES:		2.0	3.6

** For your average (mean) score divide your skills total by 10

If your average skills score is 2.5 or higher, you probably already possess enough business skills to start running a business, but you should develop an improvement plan to bring your overage average up to at least 3.0. If your score is 3.0 or higher, you definitely have most or all of the skills to start and run a business, but you will benefit by raising your score to 3.5 or above.

Next, let's see if you have the business **attitudes** to apply your knowledge and skills effectively in running your business.

8

ASSESSING YOUR ATTITUDES

As important as having sufficient knowledge and skills is to successfully running a business, the most vital attributes for an entrepreneur are **attitudes**. Your attitudes are the wellspring of motivation, innovation, adaptability, and action.

Knowledge can be acquired by reading, listening, and watching. Skills can be learned through practice and training. But attitudes can only be developed by deliberately altering your personality, core values, and beliefs—your beliefs about yourself, in particular.

Score yourself in each of the attitudes in the tables below and transfer your scores to the summary page at the end of this chapter in the same way you previously scored yourself in the knowledge and skill factors using the scoring system below:

0 = Absent (you have little or none of this attitude)
1 = Rare (this attitude is seldom evident in you)
2 = Inconsistent (this attitude comes and goes)
3 = Usual (this is your typical attitude with occasional lapses)
4 = Compelling (this attitude is your life's driving force)
5 = Exemplary (you epitomise this attitude at all times)

Circle the number in the "Score" column that corresponds to the description in each table that best describes your current level of skill in each of the ten categories that follow below in this chapter.

If in doubt, err on the side of caution and select the lower of the categories that most closely describe you.

Positivity

DESCRIPTION OF ATTITUDE	SCORE
Generally negative attitude, pessimistic, seldom upbeat or smiling	0
Optimistic about half the time, but easily discouraged or disappointed by problems and set-backs	1
Seldom discouraged, usually smiling, optimistic, and expecting good results	2
Always optimistic, even when things don't seem to be going well	3
Always optimistic, consistently encouraging others, always see the bright side, sees problems and set-backs as opportunities	4
Encouraged by every setback, failure, or calamity, knowing it brings you a step closer to success	5

Your Score: _____

Since you are the face and voice of your enterprise, your attitudes serve as the primary example for your employees, vendors, contractors, suppliers, and anyone else who represents your business to the public. In addition, your attitude is the most powerful influence on investors and lenders, and their perception of the viability of your business. It is therefore essential that you display a positive attitude at all times. **A score of 2 is the absolute minimum,** a score of 3 is preferable, and **a score of 4 or more should be your goal.**

Entrepreneurial Mindset

DESCRIPTION OF ATTITUDE	SCORE
Unwilling to work hard for long hours unless there are immediate rewards for your effort	0
Sees current job as boring, unfulfilling, pointless, or dead end, but necessary to survive, works "for the weekend"	1
Sees current job as an opportunity to acquire useful skills and knowledge for future use and/or more fruitful work	2
Deliberately cultivates opportunities to develop and improve KSAs from work activities	3
Constantly seeing and acting upon new entrepreneurial opportunities	4
Have started several successful new ventures (business, social, or charitable)	5

Your Score: _____

An entrepreneurial mindset is more than just a strong work ethic, it is a hunger to create, grow, and improve both your business and yourself as a person. As with all attitudes, your mindset establishes the tone and example for everyone associated with your business. **A score of 2 is the minimum, and a score of 4 or 5 is desirable.**

Mission-Driven

DESCRIPTION OF ATTITUDE	SCORE

Only working for a paycheck; little or no commitment to the organisation or its mission	0
Receives some satisfaction from work, but working chiefly for personal gain	1
Loves the work and would only quit if conditions or compensation became intolerable	2
Committed to organisational mission and would work for less or under worse conditions	3
So committed to the mission you would work for free	4
So committed to the mission you would pay to be involved	5

Your Score: _____

To endure the daily grind of running your own business, you must be driven by your commitment to the vision, purpose, and mission for which you founded it. It must be the reason you get out of bed in the morning, and must be strong enough to inspire your employees, customers, sources of finance to help you achieve it. **A minimum score of 2 is essential**, and **a score of 3 or more is preferable**.

However, there is a danger is becoming too fanatical about the mission of your business, so **a score above 4 could prove detrimental** to your success. If you are so devoted to the mission of your business that you would pay to work there, then you will also be inclined to "give away the store" to achieve it.

Passion, Vision, and Commitment

DESCRIPTION OF ATTITUDE	SCORE

Only working for a paycheck or other rewards; little or no passion for the work itself	0
Sees some value in the work, but doing it mostly to earn a living	1
Sees considerable value in work and derives some satisfaction from doing it	2
Deeply fulfilled by the work itself; sees it as a way to improve other people's lives	3
Considers their work a calling, feels born to do it as a vital service to humanity	4
Considers their work the most important work a human being can do	5

Your Score: _____

One of my jobs as a preteen was cleaning the restrooms in a trucking terminal—work that was menial, dirty, and often disgusting. But, one day a long-distance driver told me how much it meant to him to have a clean, inviting place to wash up after 10 hours behind the wheel and another four to six loading, unloading, and maintaining his vehicle. "It's like finding an oasis when you're dying of thirst."

That comment by a man whose name I've long forgotten changed my outlook on work. From that day forward, I've always been able to see the importance of the work I've done to the lives of the people it affects.

That's the importance of passion, vision, and commitment. It's the ability to understand the value and significance of your work to the people you're serving (vision), becoming passionate about serving them as well as possible, and committing yourself to performing that work with excellence.

As an entrepreneur, you must see your business in that way: as a vital service that improves the lives of your customers, employees, vendors, lenders, and investors. Be passionate about achieving that vision, and commit yourself to developing yourself and your business as the best way people can obtain the products and services you provide.

A score of at least 3 in this attitude is vital to the success of your business.

Devotion to Excellence

DESCRIPTION OF ATTITUDE	SCORE
Usually produces work that is of acceptable quality to boss or customer	0
Usually produces work that fully meets the expectations of boss or customer	1
Produces work that exceeds expectations of boss or customer if rewarded or recognised for it	2
Consistently produces work that exceeds expectations of boss or customer	3
Consistently strives to produce and improve upon the highest quality work available	4
Consistently strives for perfection in all work performed	5

Your Score: _____

Good enough is never good enough. Adequacy is utterly inadequate. Mediocrity is a formula for failure in business. To succeed as an entrepreneur, you must always be striving for excellence in every aspect of your business. Remember that the "miracle of economics" is that each party to a transaction is convinced they have received more from the other than they gave, so excellence makes your products and services more valuable and therefore more profitable.

A score of 3 is the minimum for this trait, and a score of 4 or 5 is preferable.

Self-Control & Discipline

DESCRIPTION OF ATTITUDE	SCORE
Has quick temper, procrastinates, disorganised, easily distracted	0
Usually controls temper, occasionally distracted, postpones difficult or unpleasant tasks	1
Usually organised and on-track, slow temper, rarely distracted, performs unpleasant duties	2
Does unpleasant tasks first, stays on-track, rarely distracted, never loses temper	3
Highly organised and prioritised, always on-time and on-task, highly efficient and effective	4
A model of self-control and discipline, almost robotic precision and efficiency	5

Your Score: _____

In a nutshell, self-control is stopping yourself from doing things you shouldn't do, and discipline is making yourself do the things you should do. An entrepreneur must have both of those qualities. Of the two, discipline is more important. It is also the most difficult.

A score of 2 is the bare minimum in this factor, but it will not sustain your business as it grows, so a score of 3 or higher should be your goal from the outset.

Conscientious & Focused

DESCRIPTION OF ATTITUDE	SCORE
Frequently lets people down, late for appointments, forgets promises	0
Usually on time and keeps promises, but occasionally side-tracked or over-promises	1
Only forgets promises, late, or lets people down if prevented by uncontrolled conditions	2
Consistently reliable, dependable, trustworthy, and punctual, rarely fails to keep promises	3
Always finds a way to keep commitments, even under dire circumstances or opposition	4
Never fails to keep an appointment or commitment, always finds a way	5

Your Score: _____

Over the last 50 years numerous studies of successful people have been conducted. In all of those studies, regardless of how success is defined—whether financial, athletic, or personal achievements—the one factor all successful people have in common is conscientiousness. In short, they are reliable, dependable, and keep their commitments.

As an entrepreneur, you must remain focused on the mission, vision, values, and goals of your business and conscientious in your work. **A score no lower than 3 is needed** in this attribute, and **a score of 4 or more is desirable.**

Personal Integrity

DESCRIPTION OF ATTITUDE	SCORE

Dishonest, corrupt, conniving, deceitful, self-centered, selfish, exploitative	0
Usually honest and trustworthy unless forced to lie, cheat, or steal for a good reason	1
Consistent moral conduct; seldom yields to temptation, anger, or desire for retribution	2
A person of character that others tell their children to be more like	3
A recognised "pillar of the community" who never knowingly harms others	4
A genuine saint with no "dirty little secrets" whatever	5

Your Score: _____

We can all point to a few dishonest, exploitative people who appear to run highly profitable businesses. But their success is usually short-lived and comes at a high psychological or spiritual cost. The widespread use of social media has made it extremely difficult to run a business unethically for very long these days. Word quickly spreads.

So, for the sake of your own emotional and spiritual well-being, as well as the reputation of yourself and your business, you must possess personal integrity and demonstration trustworthiness and sincerity in all your business dealings.

No less than a score of 2 is sufficient, and **a score of 3 or higher is essential for long-term success.**

Benevolence, Justice, and Compassion

DESCRIPTION OF ATTITUDE	SCORE

Indifferent to the difficulties, suffering, needs, or feelings of others	0
Sympathetic and helps others when able, but often lacks the resources to help	1
Helps those in need and seeks justice for others when resources and circumstances allow	2
Generous, supportive, and seeks justice for others, even when inconvenient or difficult	3
Always follows the Golden Rule, applies tough love, altruistic, seeks betterment of others	4
Christ-like at all times	5

Your Score: _____

When considering this attribute it is important not to conflate benevolence with generosity, nor compassion with sympathy. As used here, benevolence means doing what benefits all of the stakeholders in your business, so it is an exercise in balancing the needs of your customers, employees, suppliers, lenders and investors, and yourself in your decisions and actions. Similarly, compassion is action; not words or feelings. Often, compassion requires "tough love." And justice entails doing what is right, which can include allowing people to suffer the consequences of their mistakes and misdeeds.

Entrepreneurs need **a minimum score of 2** in this trait, and are **better served by a score of 3 or higher.**

Willpower

DESCRIPTION OF ATTITUDE	SCORE

Gives up when things get difficult or when facing failure, easily discouraged	0
Only gives up after repeated failures, knows when to quit	1
Only gives up if the situation becomes utterly hopeless	2
Never gives up, goes down swinging, can only be defeated but never discouraged	3
Gets back up after every defeat and tries again, sees defeat and failure as a learning process	4
Won't stop for any reason other that death itself	5

Your Score: _____

The hallmark of every successful entrepreneur is a "never say die" attitude. An entrepreneur must approach business with the conviction that failure is not an option, and that every problem, set-back, and obstacle is an opportunity to learn, grow stronger, and overcome.

An entrepreneurial mindset can be summed up as "there must be a way to prevail and I will find it somehow." And if you have the KSAs or you are diligently working to acquire them, you can have the confidence that you will, in fact, succeed.

A score of 3 or higher in willpower is therefore a must.

Attitudes Self-Assessment Summary

Congratulations! You have completed the attitudes self-assessment and can **transfer your score in each category of to the Attitudes Summary Table** on the next page, in your Self-Assessment Workbook, or to a separate sheet of paper or notebook.

Attitudes Summary Table

DESCRIPTION OF KNOWLEDGE AREA	YOUR SCORE	MIN. SCORE	IDEAL SCORE
Positive Outlook		2	4+
Entrepreneurial Mindset		2	4+
Mission-Driven		2	3-4
Passion, Vision, and Commitment		3	4+
Devotion to Excellence		3	4+
Self-Control & Discipline		2	3+
Personal Integrity		2	3+
Benevolence, Justice, and Compassion		2	3+
Willpower		3	4+
ATTITUDE TOTALS:		21	32+
**AVERAGE SCORES:		2.3	3.6

** For your average (mean) score divide your skills total by 9

If your average score in attitudes is 2.5 or higher, you probably already have strong enough attitudes to begin running a business, but you should develop an improvement plan to bring your overage average up to at least 3.0. If your score is 3.0 or higher, you definitely have most or all of the attitudes to run a business, but you will still benefit by raising your score to 3.5 or above.

Take a deep breath and release it slowly. You can even applaud yourself if you like. You've completed the KSA self-assessments. Now the real work begins. Turn to Chapter 9 to begin developing your self-improvement plan.

9

YOUR KSA IMPROVEMENT PLAN

You didn't really think you were done, did you? As important as it is to perform an objective evaluation of your KSAs, just knowing your strengths and weaknesses is only half the purpose of this exercise.

The important part is developing a clear plan to improve your KSAs, particularly in those areas that are most crucial to the success of your business.

Start by transferring your scores from the summary tables at the end of Chapters 6, 7, and 8 to the results table below:

Overall Results

KSA Section	Total Score	Average Score	Target Range*
Knowledge			2.0—4.0
Skills			2.0—4.0
Attitudes			3.5 and up
Grand Total			3.0—4.25

By comparing your average scores in each category above

and comparing them to the target ranges in the right-hand column, you can form a general idea of your current KSAs.

To understand the significance of your scores, please consider the following:

Scoring Explanation

Knowledge: With an average score of 2.0 to 4.0 you have enough general business knowledge to start a successful business, because you can hire employees or consultants to furnish you with any knowledge you currently lack. Ideally, however, you should have an average knowledge of 3.0 to 4.0 to optimise your likelihood of success. An average score much higher than 4.0 may indicate that you are too cerebral to succeed in business, since you will have a tendency to over analyse and overthink decisions.

Skills: An average score of 2.0 to 4.0 suggests that you have the business skills to start and manage a successful business, because you can also hire employees or consultants to perform tasks you may lack the skills to do yourself (e.g., tax preparation, legal advice, advertising, ...). Ideally, however, you should have an average skill level of 3.0 to 4.0 to optimise your likelihood of success and ensure that your consultants are giving you good advice. An average score much higher than 4.0 may indicate that you should be teaching business instead of running one.

Attitudes: With an average score of 3.5 or higher you have the right attitudes to start and manage a successful business. You cannot hire or rent great attitudes, because employees with great attitudes will not work long for a boss with poor attitudes or ethics. You must have great attitudes to retain employees with great attitudes.

Overall: Ideally, you should have an overall average score between 3.5 and 4.25, which means that you have a balance of KSAs that optimise your likelihood of success. An average much higher than 4.25 may indicate that you are too cerebral, too analytical, and over-zealous, which can actually be a detriment to your business.

Next Steps

Now that you have assessed your KSAs, you will need to develop an action plan to either acquire those in which you are deficient or to work around your weaknesses. The good news is that you don't have to fix everything overnight. Growth is a process and a lifelong commitment. The day you stop trying to improve your own KSAs is the day your business begins to die.

The Japanese have an approach to improvement called *kaizen*, which means "continual, incremental or gradual improvement." Unless something is malfunctioning severely, it is not necessary to make a huge change immediately, but instead to make a conscious effort to make small adjustments and improvements every day. It not only breaks the improvement process down into manageable baby-steps that can be accomplished one at a time, but it also allows you to see the effects of previous corrective efforts and be sure you're moving in the right direction before taking each new step in the process.

So, for each area (knowledge, skills, and attitudes) of the assessment, your next step is to identify **no fewer than three, nor more than five**, factors in which an improvement will be most beneficial to you and your business, and create a plan and timetable for improving it. You cannot improve everything at once, so focus your efforts on the factors that will produce the greatest impact in the next twelve months. The fewer the better.

To select your three to five highest priority areas of knowledge in which to improve, it may help to review and compare your scores for each category. Circle your score in each category in the chart that follows, so you can readily identify your relative strengths and weaknesses. Then consider how important each of those knowledge areas is to the success of your business.

Be sure to evaluate both the importance and *urgency* of each factor, since some types of knowledge may not have as great an effect on your success now as it will have later. For example, your greatest weakness might be finance, but if you already have sufficient capital to meet the present needs of your business, it may not be urgent that you acquire that knowledge now, rather than when you are preparing to expand in the future.

Knowledge

- Industry Knowledge: 0 1 2 3 4 5
- Economics Fundamentals: 0 1 2 3 4 5
- Basic Marketing Principles: 0 1 2 3 4 5
- Arithmetic Concepts: 0 1 2 3 4 5
- Probability & Statistics: 0 1 2 3 4 5
- Finance & Financial Management: 0 1 2 3 4 5
- Production & Operations Mgmt: 0 1 2 3 4 5
- Business Law: 0 1 2 3 4 5
- Psychology & Human Behaviour: 0 1 2 3 4 5

Your Knowledge Improvement Plan

Now that you have identified the knowledge categories of greatest value to you, prepare a plan for acquiring the knowledge you need most. Use bullet-points or one-sentence descriptions, if possible, but be specific. If you decide, for example that you will take a community college course in Economics, then name the college, the course number, the enrollment deadline, the beginning and ending dates of the course, whether it is online, classroom, or hybrid, its costs (tuition, books, fees, etc.), and anything you must do to prepare for the course (computer upgrade, obtain high school transcripts, or whatever). The more fully you plan for each step now, the more likely it is you will complete the process.

Use the template below to guide your thinking through the process. If you are using the workbook, five copies of the Knowledge Improvement Plan template are provided. Otherwise, you can either scan the template below or reproduce it in a text document or write it a notebook or notepad.

Knowledge Improvement Plan Template

Do YOU Have What It Takes to Run a Business?

Category: _____

Action: _____

_____

Goal: _____

_____

_____

Start Date: _____

Completion Date: _____

Estimated Cost: $_____

Preparation Required: _____

_____

_____

Steps Involved: (Check each box when completed ☑)

☐ _____

☐ _____

☐ _____

☐ _____

☐ _____

☐ _____

☐ _____

☐ _____

Using the previous example of taking a course in Economics, you would fill in the blanks in the template with information similar to that shown below that reflects your needs and the needs of your business:

Category: Economic Knowledge

Action: Complete Economics 101 at XYZ Community College in the Fall term this year

Goal: Earn a grade of B or higher, understand major economic principles, and learn how to calculate or estimate supply and demand curves, price elasticity, and profit maximising price

Start Date: 17 August 20XX

Completion Date: 19 December 20XX

Estimated Cost: $375.00**

Preparation Required: Obtain high school transcripts, backpack, notebooks and supplies, apply by 31 July 20XX, and brush up on algebra by doing problems from Algebra For Dummies

Steps Involved:

☐ Obtain high school transcripts by 15 July
☐ Apply to XYZ Community College by 31 July
☐ Buy Algebra For Dummies from Amazon by 01 Aug
☐ Register fir Economics 101 by 10 Aug
☐ Buy backpack and supplies 15 Aug
☐ Begin attending classes 17 Aug
☐ Complete course on 19 Dec

**Include all known and anticipated costs; not just the cost of the course itself. In this case the estimate includes the $40 college application fee, the $129 fee for Econ 101, the $109 textbook (including sales tax), $25 high school transcript fee, and the anticipated cost of $70 for a backpack and school supplies, rounded to the nearest $5.

Follow this pattern for each of the three to five knowledge categories you identified as being the most important to you.

When you have completed your Knowledge Improvement Plan, use the next template to create a Skills Development Plan.

Skills Improvement Plan Template

Category: _____

Action: _____

_____

Goal: _____

_____

_____

Start Date: _____

Completion Date: _____

Estimated Cost: $_____

Preparation Required: _____

_____

_____

Steps Involved: (Check each box when completed ☑)

☐ _____

☐ _____

☐ _____

☐ _____

☐ _____

☐ _____

☐ _____

☐ _____

As with the Knowledge Improvement Plan, your Skills Improvement Plan should address **not less than three** nor more than five skills for improvement. Complete the template that follows in the same way you completed the knowledge template.

Unlike knowledge, skills cannot be acquired by reading books and articles. They are only acquired by doing things. If you want to become better at maths, for example, you have to perform mathematical calculations. While there are classes that provide opportunities to practice skills you wish to improve, you may have to be more resourceful and creative to find activities that will improve your skills. Part-time jobs or volunteer work often afford such opportunities. Some hobbies, crafts, social clubs, and games can also present skill-building opportunities.

When you have completed your knowledge and skills improvement plans, take the same approach to creating a plan to improve three to five crucial attitudes.

The majority of your KSA improvement plan should focus on attitudes. With the right attitudes, you will always make a way to acquire any knowledge or skills you may lack, but with the wrong attitudes, no amount of knowledge or skill will overcome the harm they do you and your business.

So evaluate your attitudes carefully and critically. This is the time to be brutally honest with yourself. No one else has to see your attitude improvement plan, so be your own worst critic. Which of your present attitudes is the most damaging to your success? Procrastination? Indecisiveness? Bad temper? Negativity? Deceitfulness? Whatever they are, and no matter how unpleasant it may be to admit those flaws, select the three to five attitudes that will do the most to improve your chances of business success and complete the template on the next page for each of them.

Improving your attitudes will do more to enhance your likelihood of success than anything else you do.

Attitude Improvement Plan Template

Category: _____

Action: _____

_____

Goal: _____

_____

_____

Start Date: _____

Completion Date: _____

Estimated Cost: $_____

Preparation Required: _____

_____

_____

Steps Involved: (Check each box when completed ☑)

☐ _____

☐ _____

☐ _____

☐ _____

☐ _____

☐ _____

☐ _____

☐ _____

If you have completed all three improvement plans, take a moment to pat yourself on the back. Do a happy dance. In fact, give yourself a treat or reward for completing the planning process. Here's why:

By applying yourself—your time, effort, initiative, and diligence—to reading this book and completing nine to fifteen KSA improvement plans, you have demonstrated that you have the necessary motivation and commitment to succeed in business.

You can do this. You just proved it.

And you now have in your possession a blueprint or road map for success. There's only one thing left to do …

Execute the plans you just made.

Start today. You've come this far. You've laid the groundwork. So, don't delay. Put your plans into motion. Start working your way down your checklists and begin creating the exceptional manager you now know you can be.

To help you along, I've included some additional information and resources in Chapter 10 that I believe you'll find useful.

10

CONCLUSION: GO FOR IT!

Now you know what you need to do. You've done your research. You have a comprehensive business plan. You know what KSAs you already possess, the KSAs you should develop further, and the KSAs you may need to acquire from outside sources until your own are more fully developed.

It's time to get started.

Don't delay. Procrastination and indecisiveness destroys as many businesses as under-financing or poor decisions. **Do it now**. Even if you're a year or more from starting or acquiring a business, begin your self-improvement process today.

One of the things that helped me greatly in focusing my attention and efforts on the most important aspects of running a business were the quaint sayings that were commonplace back in my teens and early adulthood. I'll mention a few bits of old fashioned home-spun wisdom in hopes that some of these adages will be of help to you, as well.

"Do *something*, even if it's wrong."

Entrepreneurs must be action-oriented. Nothing is actually accomplished by thinking or talking. Everything that is ever achieved happens by *doing*. Of course, you should think and talk through every decision beforehand, but if you have the right KSAs to be a manager, then you have the tools to quickly analyse a situation, develop three or four potential solutions, run them by your trusted inner circle, and choose the one with the greatest likelihood of success. Once that's done, act immediately. Problems rarely fix themselves, so doing something is almost always better than doing nothing.

"Start where you are. Use what you have. Do what you can."

That is sage advice from the late, great tennis champion, Arthur Ashe Jr.. Start working toward your dreams right now. Don't wait until you have more skills, more money, more time, more energy, or whatever other excuse is holding you back. If you're not ready to open the doors of your business yet, then do something today that will bring you a step closer. Do what you can with what you've got to obtain whatever else you may need. And do it right now. Even baby steps are progress, so make some progress every day.

"Never, never, never give up."

Sir Winston Churchill was quite possibly the most inspirational orator in human history—a man who almost single-handedly held an island nation together whilst the most powerful war machine on earth was attempting to destroy it. His wisdom was proven by the outcome of that war, so his advice is worth following. Once you've set your goals, never give up. You may stumble and fail many times, but if you never give up, you will eventually succeed.

"Too many of us are not living our dreams because we are living our fears."

This quote by Les Brown perfectly sums up why "The mass of men lead lives of quiet desperation." The majority of people are held back by their fear of failure and disappointment from leading the rich and fulfilling lives they crave. Don't be one of them. Entrepreneurship is risk. Have the courage to take the risk of criticism and failure to accomplish what others only wish they could do..

"If you can't yet do great things, do small things in a great way."

Napoleon Hill nailed it. No one is born great. We are all born weak and helpless. Those few who achieve greatness at anything do so because they started doing small things in a great way and learned to do bigger and bigger things in that same great way. Follow their example. Whatever you're doing today to achieve your ambitions, do it in a great way.

"You must expect great things of yourself before you can do them."

Who would know better than Michael Jordan what it takes to become one of the greatest of all time? MJ didn't make his high school varsity team the first time he tried out, so he devoted nearly every waking moment afterward to becoming one of the greatest basketball players of all time, if not *the* greatest. And he understood the importance of expecting greatness of yourself. If you're not striving to be the greatest, you'll never rise above mediocrity.

"Good enough never is."

You've probably also heard that "The enemy of great is good." Mediocrity is death for any business. No customer walks into a business hoping that the products or services are barely acceptable. Your customers expect more than mediocrity, and if you don't provide them with something exceptional, few will ever come back. So don't ever settle for "good enough," unless it's only to gain time to do better.

"Fail your way to the top."

I've enjoyed some significant successes in my business ventures, but I've also had several truly spectacular failures. And it was those failures that taught me the lessons I needed to learn to create my occasional successes. People expect to succeed, otherwise they were crazy to try, so we rarely stop and analyse our successes. Instead, we simply assume we succeeded because of our brilliance and move on. But, the anguish and self-doubt of failure usually makes us think long and hard about how, when, where, and why we went wrong. Failure not only keeps us humble, but it's often the best education we can possibly get.

"The pessimist sees difficulty in opportunity. The optimist sees the opportunity in every difficulty."

Another gem from Sir Winston Churchill. Difficulty is a given. Anything and everything in life that is worth doing is difficult. Entrepreneurs train themselves to ignore the difficulties of life and see the opportunities those difficulties present. Every difficulty you face is an opportunity to grow stronger, wiser, and more capable. And the more difficult something is to accomplish, the greater the opportunity to be the only one with the courage and ability to achieve it.

"You can't *expect* more than you *inspect.*"

That's an old military saying, but it still holds true. As an entrepreneur you must stay on top of everything and verify that that people (employees, contractors, agents, suppliers, lenders, etc.) do what they agree to, and that things (supplies, equipment, furnishings, products, etc.) are what they claim to be. If you take your eye off the ball, people will take advantage of your inattention and try to rob you blind.

"Money is time."

Some famous guy had it bass-ackwards when he said, "Time is money." Unless you're a loan shark, time alone can't earn or save you money, but money can often buy you more time. A partial payment can delay a collection or repossession, for example. Money can purchase life-extending medical treatment. It can also buy time-saving technology. And time is life itself. Every minute you don't spend on some unproductive task is a bonus minute you can devote to the important matters of life: your dreams, your ambitions, and your family.

"Cash is king."

Money in your hand or bank account is almost always more useful than money that hasn't yet been paid to you. An IOU, promissory note, or an invoice can't buy much, unless you discounted it greatly for the possibility that it's uncollectible. But, with cash on hand you can often get discounts on purchases for immediate payment, or seize opportunities that others must forego due to lack of funds.

"Waste not, want not."

The largest single expense in most businesses is waste. It not the cost of labour, or supplies, or facilities, or equipment, or utilities. It's the combined cost of the wasted labour, supplies, facilities, utilities, and equipment that is the greatest single expense incurred by most businesses. Every bit of waste you can eliminate from your business is money in its bank account —money now available for growth and improvement that otherwise would have been tossed out with the rubbish.

"A penny saved is a penny earned."

When Ben Franklin said that, the US government hadn't yet invented the income tax. Nowadays a penny saved is a lot more than a penny earned. The average American business operates on a profit margin of 5% or less, and out of that 5% the federal government takes 21% in taxes and most states assess an additional 2% to 11% in franchise taxes. So, a penny saved is really only about eight-tenths of a cent. But, **that's still 20 times as much as a penny earned** that will net you less than $4/100^{th}$ of a cent. The time and effort you devote to cutting costs will pay you 20 times what you will net by increasing your revenues by the same amount.

"People often say that motivation doesn't last. Well, neither does bathing. That's why we recommend it daily."

Zig Ziglar was one of the great motivational speakers. He made a good living getting people pumped up, and he understood a vital aspect of motivation: it needs constant reinforcement. The daily grind takes a toll. It can eventually wear down even the most resilient entrepreneur, so be sure to give yourself a daily dose of motivation as you start each work day.

"In theory, there's no difference between theory and practice, but in practice there is."

Truths like this from the former Yankee catcher and manager, Yogi Berra, have become known as "Yogi-isms." They often appear at first to be *non sequiturs* until given some thought. The problem with most theories is that they assume ideal circumstances. But nothing is ideal in the real world. Reality is messy, ever-changing, unpredictable, and often illogical. So, what sounds great in theory, rarely works in actual practice. Entrepreneurs can't be idealists; they must be pragmatists. You must do what actually works; not what you wish would work in a perfect world.

Thoughts on the Normal Curve

It's likely you've heard of the "Normal" Curve, also known as the Gaussian Curve after its discoverer, the great 18th and 19th century mathematician, Johann Carl Friedrich Gauss.

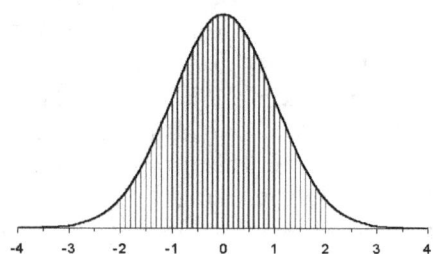

The Gaussian Curve (above) reveals that, whenever a large number of people perform a given task, their performance of that task will be distributed as follows:

- 3% will perform dismally, far below average
- 13% will perform inadequately
- 68% will perform within the average range
- 13% will perform proficiently
- 3% will perform exceptionally well

In the academic realm, the Normal Curve was used to create the old-fashioned grading scale in which the top 3% receive a "A" grade, the 13% below that get a "B," the 68% in the middle are awarded a "C," the 13% below that earn a "D," and the bottom 3% get an "F."

An Italian engineer from the late 19th century named Vilfredo Pareto independently observed that 80% of the world's wealth was amassed by about 15% of the population, that 80% of the accomplishments in any field of endeavor were achieved by roughly 15% of the those working in that discipline, and that 80% of all problems were caused by 15% of the people. From these observations he developed what he called the "80/15 Rule" that became known as the Pareto Principle after his death and is now frequently misstated as the "80/20 Rule."

The Gaussian Curve should be considered in nearly every business decision you make. It is true of your customers, your suppliers, your lenders, ... even yourself. Your performance will fall somewhere in that normal curve. For your business to succeed, you must perform the most important of your activities in that top 16% (the proficient and exceptional). And you must also strive to use only employees, contractors, or suppliers who consistently perform in that upper 16%, as well.

Unless you weed out the 84% who perform C, D, and F grade work, 80% of your successes will be produced by the top 16% of your people, and 80% of your problems will be caused by the bottom 16%.

A major consequence of the 80/15 Rule is that you will heap more work on those 16% who perform the best, and if they are not recognised, affirmed, and rewarded for their greater contributions and value to your organisation, they will grow dissatisfied and quit, leaving you with only the mediocre and slackers.

Unfortunately for business owners and managers, our government misunderstands and usually misapplies the concept of "equal pay for equal work." The government tends to insist that if two employees have the same job description, they must be made the same wage. Companies that comply with that misinterpretation invariably fail, because they end up with a workforce consisting entirely of losers.

To be sure you can compensate and retain those upper 16%

and weed out that bottom 16% and the lower half of the 68% who are merely adequate, you must develop accurate ways to measure employee and contractor performance, and build those measurements into your employment agreements and contracts together with appropriate rewards and penalties.

REMINDER: "You can't *expect* more than you *inspect.*"

Thoughts on the Learning Organisation

Everyone who achieves greatness at something, whether it's in the arts, sciences, sports, entertainment, or business, is a student of that field. The top professionals I've met in every area of life—musicians, dancers, actors, athletes, scientists, military, and business people— have not only practiced and performed their chosen trade, they have studied it purposefully, intensely, and extensively. They understand both the how and the why of every aspect of their craft.

In the early 1990s a business guru named Peter Senge coined the term "learning organisation" for businesses that encourage and reward employees for developing and enhancing their KSAs. In the 1950s a self-educated USMC veteran named Fred O'Reilly had already developed a simple, but effective way to create a learning organisation. He instituted a policy that his company would only hire entry-level employees, so that all other positions would be filled by promoting existing employees from within, unless none were qualified for the vacant job. The other side of that policy was that no employee was eligible for promotion unless he or she had trained a qualified replacement within the company.

The result of these two policies was that **every employee in the company was a learner**, and **every employee above entry level was a teacher**, trainer, and mentor. Simple, but highly effective.

That is certainly not the only way to create a learning organisation, but it can serve as a starting point for you to improve upon. If you want to grow your business, you must grow with it by constantly improving your KSAs. And your employees and contractors must also grow with your business, either by enhancing their own KSAs or being replaced by those with greater KSAs.

One of the best things you can do to create a learning organisation is to become both a **voracious reader** and a voracious writer. Not only will you set the example for others involved in your business, but the acts of reading and writing will do more to improve your analytical abilities, vocabulary, and communication skills than nearly anything else.

Remember book reports? There's a good reason they were once so popular with school teachers: they force you to think. To write a book report, you must read the book and identify its most important concepts. Then you must organise those concepts in some logical order and restate them in your own words. Those actions train you to search for major ideas, analyse those ideas, organise your thoughts, and choose the right words to express those thoughts clearly.

If you don't know where to start, below are some books I have found extremely helpful:

<u>Suggested Reading & Resources</u>:

- *The Practice of Management* (1954) by Peter F. Drucker (still the best!)
- *The Effective Executive* (1967) by Peter F. Drucker
- *Innovation & Entrepreneurship* (1985) by Peter F. Drucker
- *Managing* (1984) by Harold Geneen with Alvin Moscow
- *Dare to Launch: A Mini-MBA* (2022) by Anne Cocquyt
- *Market-Based Management*, 6th Edition (2016) by Roger J. Best
- *Good to Great* (2001) by Jim Collins
- *In Search of Excellence* (1982) by Tom Peters and Robert H. Waterman Jr.
- *Beyond Excellence 2.0* (2020) by Jim Collins
- *Competing for Advantage, 3rd Edition* (2012) by Hoskinson, Hitt, et al
- *Blue Ocean Strategy, Expanded Edition* (2015) by W. Chan Kim and Renee Mauborgne
- *First Things First* (1996) by Steven R. Covey
- *Seven Habits of Highly Effective People, 30th*

Anniversary Edition (2020) by Steven R. Covey
- *Synergy and Other Lies* (1998) by Harold Geneen and Brent Bowers
- *The Art of Demotivation* (2003) by E. L. Kersten
- *Free to Choose* (1990) by Milton Friedman
- *Economics: A Contemporary Introduction* (2016) by William A. McEachern (buy it used)
- *Economic Facts and Fallacies, 2nd Edition* (2011) by Thomas Sowell

> **NOTE:** To improve your knowledge and skills in areas like arithmetic, probability and statistics, website building, marketing, economics, financial management, accounting, business law, psychology, business writing, the "For Dummies" series of books available from Amazon are a good starting place. Don't be put off by the title. They are written specifically for people who need to learn the basics of those disciplines for practical application rather than academic theory.

Don't forget: We live in an ever-changing world. Competitors change, market conditions change, technology changes, economic conditions change, laws and regulations change, consumer attitudes and behaviours change, ... **and so must you**.

Developing, improving, and expanding your KSAs must therefore be an ongoing process. If you're not growing, your business can't grow. It will stagnate right along with you. So periodically review your KSAs in light of the changes in the world around you, and refresh your KSA improvement plan every two or three years.

The KSA improvement plan you made today is the first step in a lifelong process of personal and professional growth.

Closing Thoughts:

"If you take the easy path, life is difficult. But, if you take the difficult path, life is easy."

That ancient *samurai* saying is profound. The "easy path" is the path of merely being part of the herd, doing the least that is necessary to get by, being led by emotion and desire, dreaming but not doing. The *samurai* took the "difficult path" of extreme personal discipline, welcoming the hardship of training to perfect themselves in every way possible, and acting based on the highest ideals of compassion, righteousness, and respect for others. The "easy path" inevitably leads to a life of selfishness and indifference to others, ingratitude, strained and damaged relationships, dissatisfaction with one's circumstances, and a belief that the deck is stacked against them. The "difficult path" produces a life of accomplishment and fulfillment, gratitude even in the midst of deprivation and hardship, intimate relationships, and a deep sense of contentment.

"Entrepreneurship isn't a job; it's a calling."

A job is just work you do solely to earn money. An entrepreneur runs a business for much broader and nobler reasons. An entrepreneur works to fulfill a vision, and if that vision is accomplished it not only benefits the entrepreneur, but also the customers, employees, vendors, lenders, local community, and society as a whole.

As I said earlier, **everything of value and usefulness in our world is created by entrepreneurs**. They are the visionaries who find ways to improve human life. Governments only restrict and destroy; they do not create or innovate. Employees only perform the tasks they are assigned to do. The driving force behind all innovation, progress, and human achievement is entrepreneurs.

In the introduction to this book I mentioned the words carved in marble at the Temple of Apollo at Delphi: "*gnothi seauton*," or "know yourself." After completing your KSA assessments and KSA improvement plan, you now know yourself better than you did before. You should now know that you are called to an entrepreneur. You are the future of our world, and you are engaged in a noble calling.

Now go use your gifts and your KSAs to help create a better world!

ABOUT THE AUTHOR

Leonard J. ("Len") Pellman is a man of many parts who was blessed beyond measure with a life of opportunity and adventure. His father was a decorated hero of World War II and his mother was an immigrant from the UK who also had a vital role in the allied victory whilst serving in the British Army.

Both of his parents were deeply involved in the civil rights movement in the 1950s and 1960s, so they ensured that he frequently experienced a wide variety of cultures growing up in Southern California. For four years of his childhood his family co-managed and lived in a 22 unit "no tell" motel, where his playmates were the children of the Black, Hispanic, and Kumeyaay maids.

Childcare was rare and expensive in the 1950s, so when he was 7 his father began taking him to work in his accounting practice and giving him increasingly responsible bookkeeping tasks, like counting currency and change, preparing deposit slips, typing checks, and reconciling petty cash.

In 1967, at the age of 15, Len and an adult partner purchased a tiny, struggling moving and storage company that had been one of his father's clients for $1,000. When they bought it, the company was only licensed to transport household goods and freight from San Diego to Coronado via the ferry system. Len found a loophole in the regulations that allowed them to expand the company's operations statewide, and later nationwide.

Using his profits from that business, Len purchased two other moving companies outright and a 10% interest in a third. Over the next 10 years, Len expanded their combined operations worldwide, with offices in more than 30 countries, and gradually increased his holdings to 100% of the stock. He even started an interplanetary transportation company that was the first and only private company to ship personal property aboard the space shuttle. In 1985 he sold those businesses to a conglomerate and used the proceeds to purchase a half dozen commercial buildings and a one-third interest in a defence contracting company that operated worldwide.

In the years that followed he started a limousine service, a data processing firm, a vehicle leasing company, and a *dōjō*. In all he has started or purchased and managed 19 businesses as of this writing.

After selling all his business interests except the *dōjō* in order to devote two years to serving as a Protestant missionary, he returned to San Diego and enrolled in an MBA programme to update and expand his business knowledge and skills. Immediately upon completion of his MBA he was hired to teach undergraduate business and economics courses. Two years later, another university hired him to manage their MBA and MSM programmes, as well as to teach night classes in those programmes.

Len retired from teaching in early 2021, and devoted the majority of his time to teaching martial arts, writing, and business consulting. Now living in San Antonio, Texas, Len has since published two books on traditional Japanese martial arts and this book on entrepreneurship and management.

Having retired once briefly in the 1990s, only to discover that he hated having nothing to do other than chores, DIY projects, and getting sunburned sitting by his swimming pool, Len has vowed never to retire again as long as his health permits him to continue working. Instead, he hopes to inspire others to become entrepreneurs and enjoy the deep satisfaction he has experienced as a lifelong business owner and manager.